MW00528549

The
Vision
of God

The Vision of God

NICHOLAS OF CUSA
INTRODUCTION BY EVELYN UNDERHILL
EMMA GURNEY SALTER, TRANSLATOR

COSIMOCLASSICS

NEW YORK

The Vision of God
Cover © 2007 Cosimo, Inc.

For information, address:

Cosimo, P.O. Box 416
Old Chelsea Station
New York, NY 10113-0416

or visit our website at:
www.cosimobooks.com

The Vision of God was originally published in 1453.

Cover design by www.kerndesign.net

ISBN: 978-1-60206-326-6

How can the intellect grasp Thee,
who art infinity?... For to understand infinity
is to comprehend the incomprehensible.

—from Chapter XIII

INTRODUCTION

THE name of Nicholas of Cusa seldom appears
in histories of Christian mysticism. Yet no one
who reads with sympathy *The Vision of God*
will feel any doubt as to his right to a place
among the great teachers of the contemplative
life; and this in spite of the fact that he gives
few explicit directions as to the way in which
it may be achieved. He teaches, like his great
master St. Augustine, almost wholly by example
and allusion; persuading his readers to share
his soliloquies, infecting them with his spirit of
adoration, and so inducing in them something
of the contemplative state.

There are two distinct, but complementary
factors, which must be present in every great
work of mysticism. First, that fresh intuition
of spiritual reality, that direct experience of
God, which makes its creator a mystic; and
enables him to bring into the current religious
life the vivifying influence of a renewed contact with Eternity. Next, and hardly less
essential to his teaching office, is the element
of tradition; all that spiritual culture which

the writer has inherited from the past and
hands on to the future, and which gives him
the framework, the convention, within which
his own direct experience can be expressed.
Without this corporate tradition, the education
which he has received from his predecessors
in the spiritual life, the mystic remains a lonely
eccentric. He does not fulfil his vocation within
the chain of history; cannot communicate his
vision to other men.

In Nicholas of Cusa we find both the individual
and the corporate factor in full and balanced
development. Historically, he must be regarded
as a late descendant of the great fourteenth-
century mystics of the Rhineland and Flanders;
reproducing their characteristic combination of
transcendental speculation, humble devotion
and pastoral zeal. With them, he has been
deeply influenced by St. Augustine and Dionysius the Areopagite; and to a less extent, by
St. Bernard and St. Thomas Aquinas. More
immediately, he is a son of that New Devotion
which arose in connection with the Brothers
of the Common Life, and goes back through
their founder Gerard Groote to the mighty
Ruysbroeck. Nicholas shares with his friend
Denis the Carthusian and his contemporary
Gerlac Petersen — and, we must add, with

Thomas à Kempis, his senior by twenty years
—the inheritance of that prince among mystics.
The peculiar temper of his mysticism, its
mingling of the metaphysical and the personal, of intellectual subtlety and devotional
fervour—so characteristic of the Flemish school
at its best—witnesses to the influences which
had moulded his soul. We see in Petersen's
Fiery Soliloquy, which perhaps comes nearer to
the outlook of *The Vision of God* than any other
single contemporary writing, the working of
these same influences on another type of mind.
The sources of doctrine, the actual ingredients,
are easily recognisable: but in both, they are
fused as in a poem by the fire of mystical
passion, to form a new thing. *The Vision of
God* shows how profound was that spiritual
craving, and how deep the impression of that
early formation, which together made a busy
ecclesiastic incessantly concerned with admini-
stration and reform, the secret companion of
St. Augustine and the Areopagite.

For Nicholas of Cusa was no specialist. He
lived towards God on every side of a rich and
powerful personality: as scholar and philo-
sopher, as churchman and reformer, he is one
of the greatest figures of the fifteenth century.
In his view, and that of all the best among

his contemporaries, the Christian religion of
that day had "degenerated into an appearance." We shall not fully understand the
rapture and confidence of the soliloquies which
form the greater and most precious part of his
wonderful little book, unless we realise the life
of incessant and largely disheartening struggle
against corruption and apathy to which their
writer was committed; and the consequent
relation between his inner vision and his outer
life. These are not the agreeable meditations
of a leisured piety; but the support of a man
weighed down by responsibility, whose varied
and exacting duties were performed under that
"gaze of God" of which he writes.

The genuine mystic has no desire for pub-
licity. His longing is to keep "his secret to
himself"; and where he is persuaded to speak
of that which he knows, he most often does so
for the benefit of individuals or groups with
whom he is in sympathy. Thus many of the
masterpieces of mystical literature are in the
nature of personal communications; from the
famous Letter to Timothy of Dionysius the
Areopagite, to the works which St. Teresa
composed for her nuns, and the great French
directors for their penitents. *The Vision of God*
falls within this class. We know that it was

addressed to the prior and monks of the re-
formed Benedictine Abbey of Tegernsee; a
devout and studious community, with whom
Nicholas had spent two happy days in June
1452. His conversation at this time awoke such
"new longings" in the monks that they begged
him to return and give them further instruc-
tion in the contemplative life; and he seems
from this time on to have acted as their
spiritual director. Through their prior, Bernard de Waging, author of the *Laudatorium
Doctæ Igorantiæ*, and an eager student of
Nicholas of Cusa's work, the brothers were
already acquainted with the principles of
mystical theology; and had taken an active
part in the learned discussions then in progress
as to the nature of that "ignorance which is
knowledge" described by Dionysius the Areopagite. But now they desired to pass from
theory to actuality. *The Vision of God*—which
rapidly became the most popular of the great
Cardinal's writings—was written for the purpose of initiating them into that mystical experience which they had so eagerly discussed
from outside. In a letter to the Community,
which fortunately survives, Nicholas says that
he is sending to the abbey a picture and a
little book; which will together introduce his

pupils into the veritable practice of Mystical Theology—in other words, will teach them to realise the Presence of God. Thus, in reading the *Vision* we should ever have in mind the picture which is described in the Preface; that "icon," or image of the Omnivoyant, on which the whole treatise is really a commentary. Its true meaning will only begin to show itself, in so far as we place ourselves beside those for whom it was written, and use it as they are told to do. Then we shall discover something of its author's secret: the device by which he brings his pupils to a certain vision of God, by showing them, first from one angle and then from another, the gaze of the Eternal ever bent upon each contemplating soul.

For the peculiar mark of this book is that, unlike many mystical writings, it centres the whole of its teaching on the all-seeing reality and prevenience of God; and not on the methods by which the soul attains Him. Nicholas of Cusa agrees with Gerlac Petersen that "It is not enough to know by estimation merely, but we must know by experience, that the soul looketh upon Him who looketh at all things past, present and to come at one glance." God, for Nicholas, is "in very truth an Unlimited Sight." The Absolute Glance falls equally, simultaneously, and unflickeringly on all. Within this Perfect Vision the small life of man is lived; it conditions his limited spiritual experience. Only because God first looks at him, can man desire to look at God; for the finite in all its degrees is enfolded and conditioned by the Infinite.

"Thy look is Thy being . . . I am, because Thou dost look at me . . . if Thou didst turn Thy glance from me, I should cease to be!"

In these strongly Augustinian thoughts and phrases Nicholas gives us the very essence of his mysticism. He is sure that the foundation of all sane and creaturely spirituality abides in this truth; that our contemplation of God exists within, and is conditioned by God's contemplation of us. Eternal Life is that "blessed vision wherewith the Infinite God looketh into the deeps of man's soul; and in so looking vivifieth it by a communication of love." This gaze of God, at once universal and particular, is perfect and unchanging. His pity and His glance are one, and never leave us during our whole lives. But at each stage of our spiritual growth our always imperfect vision of Him inevitably changes, and He seems to us other than He was before. Thus it is that "Thine infinite goodness maketh Thee seem subject to mutability; since Thou dost never desert Thy creatures, which *are* subject to mutability." Man, as it were, moving about his interior castle, meets the single gaze of the Omnivoyant from many different points of view: a thought which might help us to solve some of the problems of comparative religion, and extend a more humble charity to those who see from another angle than ourselves.

Thus we may say that the very heart of Nicholas's mysticism is the conviction of the absolute priority of God's action over the soul's action. All possibilities inhere in Him; He is Pure Potency and Pure Act. But hardly less fundamental to his teaching is that conception of God's utter transcendence to which he gives in his soliloquies such magnificent expression. Students of Rudolf Otto's philosophy will here notice with interest the many identities between his thought and that of Nicholas of Cusa. Both are dominated by that intense conviction of the mysterious over-plus of the Godhead, and the merely approximate character of even our greatest efforts to conceive it, which transforms the whole spiritual outlook of those to whom it comes. By the path of intellectual speculation, or by the shorter and more direct method of "loving

ascent," man, says Nicholas, may reach that
" wall of Paradise " beyond which is the
dwelling-place of God. But here human reason
fails: and obscure contemplation—the "wisdom
which is ignorance"—must take its place. "A
high wall separates Thee from all that can
possibly be said or thought of Thee!" For the
Being of God, as Ruysbroeck had said of Him,
abides in a world that is "in no wise." This sense
of the supra-rational aspect of Deity has pursued
a chequered course through Christian history.
Colouring the mysticism of St. Augustine and
Dionysius the Areopagite, and developed with
splendour by St. John Chrysostom, it reappears
in the great mystical writers of the fourteenth
century; especially those who have been influenced by the powerful genius of Meister
Eckhart. "Of God Himself can no man think,"
said the English author of *The Cloud of Un-
knowing*; "He dwells," says Ruysbroeck, in "a
dim silence where all lovers lose themselves."
"Thou in Thy goodness," says Nicholas, "dost
let the blind speak of Thy Light." The cer-
tainty that men cannot know the Absolute
One as He is, and a consequent sense of
the symbolic nature of all our religious conceptions, are thoughts never far from his
mind. Man's reason, he says boldly, can only

conceive of God in human ways. The theology of the lion, the eagle and the ox would display similar limitations. Only by overpassing that farthest boundary of thought where all contraries coincide, and the apparent antinomies of man's experience are resolved, can we reach the place "beyond the wall of Paradise"—a sphere transcending all our conceptions—where by an obscure and loving intuition God in His Eternity is contemplated without veils.

"O my God, the Absolute and Eternal; it is beyond the Present and the Past that Thou dost exist and utter speech!"

Thus it follows that we cannot hope to apprehend the invisible God, the Absolute Love, save in His self-revelation. So we are led from our contemplation of the gaze of God transcending all creatures and including them in His "Eternal Now," to the revelation of God as immanent in creatures; since His essence penetrates all things, and through them He draws man's spirit to Himself—another wall of paradox, behind which dwells His unsearchable Truth. This theme leads Nicholas to meditate upon the Trinity as a "Threefold Love"; and then upon the incarnation of Christ, "the loveableness of God." In his treatment of the doctrine of the Trinity, the influence of Ruysbroeck is strongly marked. The beautiful soliloquies and prayers incorporated in these closing chapters are a valuable addition to the literature of Christo-centric devotion. In them the great Cardinal discloses the secret of his arduous and devoted life. Often reminiscent of St. Augustine, they are marked by their author's peculiar blend of metaphysical passion and intimate love; and possess in an eminent degree the power of the poet-mystic, to lift those who yield to their influence to an experience beyond the span of human speech, where the soul tastes of that Reality which it may never comprehend.

EVELYN UNDERHILL.

BIOGRAPHICAL NOTE

The author of the *De Visione Dei* was born in 1401 at Cues (Cusa) on the Moselle, in the diocese of Trier. His father was a boatman named Krebs; Khrypffs and other variants of the name are found. The family were fairly well off; they joined later with Nicholas in endowing a hospice in their native place. The boy's early studious tastes may perhaps have recommended him to the notice of Count Ulric von Manderscheid; at any rate, he went to be educated under the Brethren of the Common Life at Deventer in Holland, whither Thomas à Kempis as a boy had preceded him some twenty years earlier. Of the life at Deventer Thomas wrote afterward with affection, and the atmosphere of mysticism prevalent there would have been congenial to Nicholas also.

At the age of sixteen, Nicholas went on to the University of Heidelberg, thence in October 1417 to that of Padua, where he studied law, taking the degree of Doctor in Canon Law in 1423. Here was stimulated his keen interest in varied studies—Greek, astronomy, mathe-

matics, statics and dynamics, and map-making
—which afterwards found expression in his *De
Conjecturis*, *De Staticis Experimentis*, *De Ludo
Globi*, and other works. He was in advance
of many of the ideas of his time—for instance,
he was convinced of the earth's motion, and
proposed (in 1436) a reform of the calendar
on lines resembling those adopted later under
Gregory.

In 1423 or 1424, Nicholas was in Rome.
The loss of a law-suit in which he was pleading
was said by a later adversary to have induced
him to leave the Bar; this seems improbable.
From whatever cause, he did decide to take
Orders, and proceeded to Cologne for his
theological course, his diocesan helping to
finance him, and, before he was priested,
giving him a canonry.

In 1426, Nicholas became acquainted with
the Cardinal Legate, Giordano Orsini, who
made him his secretary. In the cardinal's circle
he met Italian humanists, and corresponded
with them about classical manuscripts at Cologne. Nicholas discovered some of Plautus
hitherto unknown, and himself became a
collector, ably collating and criticising the
manuscripts. He had several translations made
of Plato, and was all his life a great reader.

He studied in Greek the works of the Pseudo-
Dionysius the Areopagite — the writer who,
with Saint Augustine, influenced him most,
and from whom he borrows freely. He was
also greatly interested in the new art of printing.
But, in contrast with many Renaissance
humanists, Nicholas remained true to Christian
faith and morals.

The air at this time was full of general ideas
of reform, and much was hoped from the
Council of Basle, then sitting. Nicholas attended
it on behalf of his patron, Ulric. He embodied
a scheme for harmony between Church and
Empire, and unity in the Church, in his *De
Concordantia Catholica*, which, at the end of
1433, he set before the Council. In it he also
discussed the reconciliation of the Imperial
power with that of the princes, and maintained
that the authority of Councils General was
superior to the Pope's.[1] Nicholas hoped that
his *Concordantia* would help to win over the
Hussites, with whom the Council was then
treating. But although, in 1433 and again in
1436, reunion seemed imminent, negotiations
were still continuing in 1464, when the Pope
appointed Nicholas as one of two judges on

[1] In this work, too, he exposed the pretended "Donation
of Constantine."

the question, a consistory being held only two months before his death.

No reforms followed on the Council of Basle, and as time went on, Nicholas began to lose faith in it, owing to its divisions and wrong-headedness; he saw that, in this instance at any rate, his conciliar theories failed in practice. He may have been drawn towards Eugenius by some of his Italian friends, and because the Pope seemed more likely to effect the reconciliation with the Greek Church, which was very near his heart. His much criticised action in finally throwing over the Council for the Pope, in the autumn of 1435, may perhaps be thus explained. Æneas Sylvius Piccolomini, afterward Pope Pius II., with whom he had become friends at the Council, severely blamed his conduct at first, but subsequently took the same line himself.

In the spring of 1437, Nicholas, with two others, went as envoy to the Greek emperor and patriarch at Constantinople, sailing back with them in November; the Pope then met them to discuss reunion at the Council of Florence. Eugenius had meanwhile dissolved the Basle Council, which elected an anti-Pope, Felix V. During the next ten years, Rome and Basle each tried to win over to its own side the

German Electors, who professed neutrality. Eugenius sent Nicholas to Germany on his behalf, where his powerful public speeches had great effect, and won for him from Æneas Sylvius the title of the "Hercules of the Eugenians." On the Pope's death in 1447, his successor, the humanist, Nicholas V., was recognised by all, and the schism ended. Pope Nicholas confirmed his namesake in the Archdeaconry of Brabant, which Eugenius had conferred on him, and created him Bishop of Brixen,[1] and Cardinal of San Pietro in Vincoli, in January 1449. He received the hat from the Pope a year later.

At the end of 1450, the Pope sent Nicholas as legate to "Germany, Bohemia, and the adjacent countries." His mandate was to work for peace, and reform of doctrine and morals; to hold provincial councils, and visit monasteries. The Cardinal travelled with a humble train only, and had a great reception, as the herald of the long-desired reforms and, above all, as a fellow-countryman. His personality and his eloquence also attracted men. He met, however, with some opposition from the enemies of reform. He preached chiefly in German, showing that true reform must begin with

[1] In the Tyrol. Now Bressanone.

inward religion, and reproving superstitions, licentiousness, simony, and other abuses. Many of his German sermons survive.

The Pope wished to send Nicholas to England to try and bring about peace between that country and France, but he never went—perhaps because another Cardinal did so, and also because of the claims of his diocese, Brixen, which he had hitherto been unable to visit, but for which he now set out (March 1452). The Bishop found it in a bad state, superstition being rampant among the peasants, and immorality among the clergy, while many of the Religious Houses were very laxly administered. In spite of the difficulty of assembling clergy in such mountainous country, Nicholas held diocesan synods at Brixen in 1453, 1455, and 1457. From the first, he was forced into conflict with the Archduke Sigismund over his episcopal dues and temporal powers. In a long, weary struggle with a recalcitrant abbess, who flatly refused any reform in her convent for ladies of noble Tyrolean families, the Archduke supported the abbess; though deposed by Papal Bull in 1454, she only resigned in 1459. This was but the most vexatious of several similar contests.

In 1458, Nicholas was in Rome for the

conclave which elected Æneas Sylvius Pope, and the following year, in the Pope's absence, he acted as Governor of Rome and the Papal States, with conspicuous success. The continued disputes with Sigismund finally culminated in a complete rupture, and the Bishop left the diocese for good, the Archduke having imprisoned and robbed him (Easter 1460), and even threatened his life. Pius II. in consequence laid the district under an interdict, as his predecessor, Calixtus, had also done: it lasted four years, and was only removed in August 1464, after the Emperor Frederick III. had intervened to make peace, in view of the proposed Crusade against the Turks. By a sad irony, Nicholas had died a few days before, on 11 August, at Todi, in Umbria, on his way to join the Pope.

He was buried in his titular church in Rome, but his heart was sent to the chapel of the hospice which he had recently founded at Cues for the accommodation of thirty-three poor men, over fifty years of age. This still exists, and contains his valuable library. Nicholas also endowed bursaries for twenty young students.

During the years of troubled rule of his

diocese, the Cardinal's chief solace had been study and meditation, and intercourse with devout Religious, among whom the Benedictines of Tegernsee came first. They had appreciated his great philosophical work, the *De Docta Ignorantia*, of 1440, and to them, in response to a request for a method of contemplation, he sent, in December 1453, the *De Visione Dei*, which he dedicated to them. In both these works, Nicholas sets out to prove that man's intellect cannot comprehend God, that his ultimate knowledge is to recognise his own ignorance: the conclusion, however, is not merely negative or agnostic, as he proceeds to show how faith, mystic vision, intuition, can unite with the Trinity. The reconciliation of all contradictions in God is the keynote of his teaching. He uses the words *complicatio* and *explicatio* to express the relation of the world to God, the former implying that all exists in God, the latter, that He is in all.[1] This, and other of his assertions, laid Nicholas open to the charge of pantheism, but he saves himself by pointing out that God transcends both "complication" and "explication" alike, in a manner beyond our reason. His devotion to the Person of Christ, especially in His aspect

[1] But sometimes, as Falckenberg points out, he uses *complicatio* for "identity," *explicatio* for "otherness."

of Mediator, which gained him the title of *Doctor Christianus*, comes out very beautifully in the *De Visione Dei*, and it is to such fervent devotional passages, often occurring toward the end of chapters, that the reader will probably feel most drawn. A study of his mysticism will be found on pp. vii to xvii.

In the transition period between Mediaeval Scholasticism and Renaissance Neo-Platonism Nicholas holds an important place. He shows traces of many influences, and himself in turn influenced many thinkers. As a writer, his style is cumbrous, and given to repetitions: he had himself deplored the defects of his Latinity.

Nicholas's dominant idea of the reconciliation of opposites was not confined to his philosophy. He believed that Islam might be converted by the pen rather than by the sword. While in Constantinople, he had studied the Koran in a translation, and when, in 1461, Pius asked him to supply a refutation of Mahomet, he compiled his *Cribratio Alchoran*, in which he endeavoured to show that parts of the Koran are true, and confirm the Gospels, while exposing the errors of the remainder. Elsewhere he had written: "Holy Scripture and the philosophers have said the same thing in different terms." With the same ideal in view, he attempted in his *De Pace Fidei* to overcome the objections of pagans and heretics to the Faith. These attempts of Nicholas may not carry conviction, but one must respect the generous spirit in which he made them, and wish that it could have survived to influence the religious contest of the following century.

.   .   .   .   .

THIS translation is made from the text of Nicholas' Latin works printed at Basle in 1565. It has been compared with the admirably lucid French version of Dr. E. Vansteenberghe,[1] and with the seventeenth century English rendering of Giles Randall.[2] The latter, besides not being quite complete, is difficult of access: the British Museum copy is one of the rare Thomason Tracts.

I wish to express my great indebtedness to Miss Evelyn Underhill, for .contributing a study of the mysticism of Nicholas, for suggestions in translating, and for calling my attention to similarities between the *De Visione Dei* and Dionÿsius. I am also most grateful to the Rev. Leslie Walker, S.J.,

[1] *La Vision de Dieu.* (Museum Lessianum. 1925.)
[2] *The Single Eye, entituled the Vision of God.* (London. 1646.) Randall, in his introductory Epistle, remarks: "There is no true living knowledge of God within us till He be in us formed in the Face of Jesus Christ. This is the divine argument of this little work selected and culled out of the most elaborate pieces of that learned Dr. Cusanus, whose argument herein is chiefly and only to shadow forth unto thee the being and existence of the Infinite God with and in the finite."

who was so good as to let me consult him about
scholastic terms, and to read the proofs. For my
brief biographical sketch I have relied on Dr.
E. Vansteenberghe's masterly work, *Le Cardinal
Nicolas de Cusa* (Paris. 1920), which gives a very
full bibliography, and on an article on Nicholas
in the *Church Quarterly Review* (April 1906), and
another in the *Dublin Review* (October 1906).

E. G. S.

CONTENTS

CONTENTS

THE VISION OF GOD
· OR
THE ICON[1]

THE BOOK OF THE MOST REVEREND FATHER
AND LORD IN CHRIST, THE LORD NICHOLAS OF
CUSA, CARDINAL-PRIEST OF SAINT PETER IN
CHAINS, BISHOP OF BRIXEN, TO THE ABBOT AND
BRETHREN OF TEGERNSEE, CONCERNING THE
VISION OF GOD, OR THE ICON.[1]

I WILL now show you, dearest brethren, as I
promised you, an easy path [2] unto mystical
theology.[3] For, knowing you to be led by zeal
for God, I think you worthy of the opening
up of this treasure, as assuredly very precious
and most fruitful. And first I pray the Almighty

[1] *Visio* has been translated "vision" in the title, and elsewhere, especially in passages referring to the Beatific Vision:
in the earlier chapters, which treat mostly of God's looking
upon man, both *visio* and *visus* are usually rendered by such
words as "sight," "gaze," "regard," or "glance," which
seem more clearly to convey the meaning.

[2] *Facilitatem.*

[3] Mystical theology is the usual term, as e.g. in St. Teresa,
for the soul's unmediated knowledge of God. Nicholas returns
to this idea in chap. xxiv., p. 125: "What is easier than to
believe in God? What is sweeter than to love Him?"

I

to give me utterance, and the heavenly Word who alone can express Himself, that I may be able, as ye can receive it, to relate the marvels of revelation, which are beyond all sight of our eyes, our reason, and our understanding. I will endeavour by a very simple and common-place method to lead you by experience into the divine darkness; wherein while ye abide ye shall perceive present with you the light inaccessible, and shall each endeavour, in the measure that God shall grant him, to draw ever nearer thereunto, and to partake here, by a sweetest foretaste, of that feast of everlasting bliss, whereunto we are called in the word of life, through the gospel of Christ, who is blessed for ever.

PREFACE

IF I strive in human fashion to transport you
to things divine, I must needs use a comparison
of some kind. Now among men's works I have
found no image better suited to our purpose
than that of an image which is omnivoyant
—its face, by the painter's cunning art, being
made to appear as though looking on all
around it. There are many excellent pictures
of such faces—for example, that of the archeress
in the market-place of Nuremberg; that by the
eminent painter, Roger,[1] in his priceless picture in the governor's house [2] at Brussels; the
Veronica in my chapel at Coblenz, and, in the
castle of Brixen, the angel holding the arms
of the Church, and many others elsewhere.
Yet, lest ye should fail in the exercise, which
requireth a figure of this description to be
looked upon, I send for your indulgence such
a picture as I have been able to procure,
setting forth the figure of an omnivoyant, and
this I call the icon of God.

[1] Presumably Roger van der Weyden. (1400–64.)
[2] *Pretorium.* Probably the Hôtel de Ville.

3

This picture, brethren, ye shall set up in
some place, let us say, on a north wall, and
shall stand round it, a little way off, and look
upon it. And each of you shall find that, from
whatsoever quarter he regardeth it, it looketh
upon him as if it looked on none other. And
it shall seem to a brother standing to eastward as if that face looketh toward the east,
while one to southward shall think it looketh
toward the south, and one to westward, toward
the west. First, then, ye will marvel how it can
be that the face should look on all and each
at the same time. For the imagination of him
standing to eastward cannot conceive the gaze
of the icon to be turned unto any other quarter,
such as west or south. Then let the brother
who stood to eastward place himself to westward and he will find its gaze fastened on him
in the west just as it was afore in the east. And,
as he knoweth the icon to be fixed and un-
moved, he will marvel at the motion of its
immoveable gaze.

If now, while fixing his eye on the icon, he
walk from west to east, he will find that its
gaze continuously goeth along with him, and
if he return from east to west, in like manner
it will not leave him. Then will he marvel
how, being motionless, it moveth, nor will his

imagination be able to conceive that it should
also move in like manner with one going in a
contrary direction to himself. If he wish to
experiment on this, he will cause one of his
brethren to cross over from east to west, still
looking on the icon, while he himself moveth
from west to east; and he will ask the other as
they meet if the gaze of the icon turn continuously with him; he will hear that it doth
move in a contrary direction, even as with
himself, and he will believe him. But, had he
not believed him, he could not have conceived
this to be possible. So by his brother's showing
he will come to know that the picture's face
keepeth in sight all as they go on their way,
though it be in contrary directions; and thus
he will prove that that countenance, though
motionless, is turned to east in the same way
that it is simultaneously to west, and in the
same way to north and to south, and alike
to one particular place and to all objects at
once, whereby it regardeth a single movement
even as it regardeth all together. And while
he observeth how that gaze never quitteth any,
he seeth that it taketh such diligent care of
each one who findeth himself observed as
though it cared only for him, and for no other,
and this to such a degree that one on whom it

resteth cannot even conceive that it should take care of any other. He will also see that it taketh the same most diligent care of the least of creatures as of the greatest, and of the whole universe.

'Tis by means of this perceptible image that I purpose to uplift you, my most loving brethren, by a certain devotional exercise, unto mystical Theology, premising three things that be serviceable thereunto.

CHAPTER I

THAT THE PERFECTION OF THE IMAGE IS VERIFIED OF GOD THE SUPREMELY PERFECT

IN the first place, I think, it should be pre-supposed that there is nothing which seemeth proper to the gaze of the icon of God which doth not more really exist in the veritable gaze of God Himself. For God, who is the very summit of all perfection, and greater than can be conceived, is called Θεός from this very fact that He beholdeth all things. Wherefore, if the countenance portrayed in a picture can seem to look upon each and all at one and the same time, this faculty (since it is the perfection of seeing) must no less really pertain unto the reality than it doth apparently unto the icon or appearance. For if the sight of one man is keener than that of another among us, if one will with difficulty distinguish objects near him, while another can make out those at a distance, if one perceive

7

an object slowly, the other more quickly—
there is no doubt but that Absolute Sight,
whence all sight springeth, surpasseth in keenness, in speed, and in strength the sight of all
who actually see and who can become capable
of sight.

For, if I examine sight in the abstract, which
I have dissociated in my mind from all eyes
and bodily organs, and consider how abstract
sight in its limited [1] state—that is, as sight in
seeing persons—is narrowed down to time and
place, to particular objects, and to other like
conditions, while sight in the abstract is in like
manner withdrawn from these conditions, and
absolute, then I well perceive 'tis not of the
essence of sight to behold one object more
than another, although it inhereth in sight,
in its limited state, to be unable to look on
more than one thing at a time, or upon all
things absolutely. But God is the true Unlimited Sight, and He is not inferior to sight
in the abstract as it can be conceived by the
intellect, but is beyond all comparison more
perfect. Wherefore the apparent vision of the
icon cannot so closely approach the supreme
excellence of Absolute Sight as our abstract

---

[1] *Contractus, contractio* are usually rendered "limited,"
"limitation," or "limiting" when the sense is active.

conception. And so there can be no doubt that whatever seemeth to exist in that image the same doth really and supremely exist in Absolute Sight.

CHAPTER II

THAT ABSOLUTE SIGHT EMBRACETH ALL MODES OF SEEING

FOLLOWING on these considerations thou mayest perceive sight to differ in those who see by reason of its varied forms of limitation. For our sight followeth the affections of our eye and mind, and thus a man's looks are now loving and glad, anon sad and wrathful; first the looks of a child, later, of a man; finally, grave, and as of an aged man. But sight that is freed from[1] all limitation embraceth at one and the same time each and every mode of seeing, as being the most adequate measure of all sights, and their truest pattern. For without Absolute Sight there can be no limited sight; it embraceth in itself all modes of seeing, all and each alike, and abideth entirely freed from all variation. All limited modes of seeing exist without limitation in Absolute Sight. For every limitation existeth in the Absolute, because

[1] *Absolutus a.* Recurs constantly; translated as above throughout.

Absolute Sight is the limiting of limitations, limiting not being limitable. Wherefore limiting pure and simple coincideth with [1] the Absolute. For without limiting naught is limited, and thus Absolute Sight existeth in all sight, because through it all limited sight existeth, and without it is utterly unable to exist.

[1] *Coincidit.* Or, "is one with." Recurs constantly; translated in one or other of these two ways throughout.

CHAPTER III

THAT THE ATTRIBUTES OF GOD ARE NOT REALLY DIFFERENT

THOU mayest in consequence remark how all attributes assigned to God cannot differ in reality, by reason of the perfect simplicity [1] of God, although we in divers ways use of God divers words. But God, being the Absolute Ground of all formal natures, embraceth in Himself all natures. Whence, although we attribute to God sight, hearing, taste, smell, touch, sense, reason and intellect, and so forth, according unto the divers significations of each word, yet in Him sight is not other than hearing, or tasting, or smelling, or touching, or feeling, or understanding. And so all Theology is said to be stablished in a circle, because any one of His attributes is affirmed of another, and to have is with God to be, and to move is to stand, and to run is to rest, and so with the other attributes. Thus, although

[1] Or, "onefoldedness."

12

in one sense we attribute unto Him movement and in another rest, yet because He is Himself the Absolute Ground, in which all otherness [1] is unity, and all diversity is identity, that diversity which is not identity proper, to wit, diversity as we understand it, cannot exist in God.

[1] *Alteritas.* So translated throughout.

CHAPTER IV

THAT THE GAZE OF GOD IS CALLED PROVIDENCE, GRACE, AND LIFE ETERNAL

APPROACH thee now, brother contemplative, unto the icon of God, and place thyself first to the east thereof, then to the south, and finally to the west. Then, because its glance regardeth thee alike in each position, and leaveth thee not whithersoever thou goest, a questioning will arise in thee and thou wilt stir it up, saying: Lord, in this image of Thee I now behold Thy providence by a certain experience of sense. For if Thou leavest not me, who am the vilest of men, never and to none wilt Thou be lacking. For Thou art present to all and to each, even as to those same, all and each, is present the Being without whom they cannot exist. For Thou, the Absolute Being of all, art as entirely present to all as though Thou hadst no care for any other. And this befalleth because there is none that doth not prefer its own being to all others,

and its own mode of being to that of all others,
and so defendeth its own being as that it would
rather allow the being of all others to go to
perdition than its own. Even so, Thou, Lord,
dost regard every living thing in such wise
that none of them can conceive that Thou
hast any other care but that it alone should
exist, in the best mode possible to it, and that
each thinketh all other existing things exist
for the sole purpose of serving this end, namely,
the best state of him whom Thou beholdest.

Thou dost not, Lord, permit me to conceive
by any imagining whatsoever that Thou, Lord,
lovest aught else more than me; since Thy
regard leaveth not me, me only. And, since
where the eye is, there is love, I prove by
experience that Thou lovest me because Thine
eyes are so attentively upon me, Thy poor
little servant. Lord, Thy glance is love. And
just as Thy gaze beholdeth me so attentively
that it never turneth aside from me, even so
is it with Thy love. And since 'tis deathless,
it abideth ever with me, and Thy love, Lord,
is naught else but Thy very Self, who lovest
me. Hence Thou art ever with me, Lord;
Thou desertest me not, Lord; on all sides
Thou guardest me, for that Thou takest most
diligent care for me. Thy Being, Lord, letteth

not go of my being. I exist in that measure
in which Thou art with me, and, since Thy
look is Thy being, I am because Thou dost
look at me, and if Thou didst turn Thy glance
from me I should cease to be.

But I know that Thy glance is that supreme
Goodness which cannot fail to communicate
itself to all able to receive it. Thou, therefore,
canst never let me go so long as I am able to
receive Thee. Wherefore it behoveth me to
make myself, in so far as I can, ever more
able to receive Thee. But I know that the
capacity which maketh union possible is naught
else save likeness. And incapacity springeth
from lack of likeness. If, therefore, I have
rendered myself by all possible means like unto
Thy goodness, then, according to the degree
of that likeness, I shall be capable of the truth.

Lord, Thou hast given me my being, of such
a nature that it can make itself continuously
more able to receive Thy grace and goodness.
And this power, which I have of Thee, wherein
I possess a living image of Thine almighty
power, is freewill. By this I can either enlarge
or restrict my capacity for Thy grace. The
enlarging is by conformity with Thee, when
I strive to be good because Thou art good, to
be just because Thou art just, to be merciful

because Thou art merciful; when all my endeavour is turned toward Thee because all
Thy endeavour is turned toward me; when I
look unto Thee alone with all my attention,
nor ever turn aside the eyes of my mind,
because Thou dost enfold me with Thy con-
stant regard; when I direct my love toward
Thee alone because Thou, who art Love's self,
hast turned Thee toward me alone. And what,
Lord, is my life, save that embrace wherein
Thy delightsome sweetness doth so lovingly
enfold me? I love my life supremely because
Thou art my life's sweetness.

Now I behold as in a mirror, in an icon, in
a riddle,[1] life eternal, for that is naught other
than that blessed regard wherewith Thou
never ceasest most lovingly to behold me, yea,
even the secret places of my soul. With Thee,
to behold is to give life; 'tis unceasingly to
impart sweetest love of Thee; 'tis to inflame
me to love of Thee by love's imparting, and
to feed me by inflaming, and by feeding to
kindle my yearnings, and by kindling to make
me drink of the dew of gladness, and by
drinking to infuse in me a fountain of life, and
by infusing to make it increase and endure.
'Tis to cause me to share Thine immortality,

---

[1] *In enigmate* (1 Cor. xiii. 12).

to endow me with the glory imperishable of
Thy heavenly and most high and most mighty
kingdom, 'tis to make me partaker of that
inheritance which is only of Thy Son, to
stablish me in possession of eternal bliss. There
is the source of all delights that can be desired;
not only can naught better be thought out by
men and angels, but naught better can exist
in any mode of being! For it is the absolute
maximum of every rational desire, than which
a greater cannot be.

CHAPTER V

THAT SIGHT IS TASTING, SEEKING, PITYING, AND ACTING [1]

O HOW great and manifold is Thy sweetness which Thou hast hidden up for them that fear Thee! It is a treasure that may not be unfolded, in the joy of fullest gladness. For to taste that Thy sweetness is by the touch of experience to lay hold on the sweetness of all delights at its source, 'tis in Thy wisdom to attain unto the reason of all things desirable. To behold Absolute Reason, which is the reason of all things,[2] is naught else than in mind to taste Thee, O God, since Thou art very Sweetness, the Being of life, and intellect. What else, Lord, is Thy seeing, when Thou beholdest me with pitying eye, than that Thou art seen of me? In beholding me Thou givest Thyself to be seen of me, Thou who art a hidden God. None can see Thee save in so far as Thou

[1] This heading is taken from the Cues MS. The printed editions repeat the heading of chap. iv. by mistake. (La Vision de Dieu, p. 18, note 1.)
[2] Or, "the absolute Why and Wherefore which is the Why and Wherefore of all things."

grantest a sight of Thyself, nor is that sight aught else than Thy seeing him that seeth Thee.

I perceive, Lord, in this image of Thee how ready Thou art to show Thy face unto all that seek Thee, for never dost Thou close Thine eyes, never dost Thou turn them away. And albeit I turn me away from Thee when I turn me utterly to some other thing, yet for all this dost Thou never move Thine eyes nor Thy glance. If Thou beholdest me not with the eye of grace, the fault is mine, who have cut me off from Thee, by turning aside, and by turning round [1] to some other thing which I prefer before Thee; yet even so dost Thou not turn Thee utterly away, but Thy mercy followeth me, that, should I at any time be fain to turn unto Thee again, I may be capable of grace. If Thou regardest me not, 'tis because I regard not Thee, but reject and despise Thee.

O infinite Pity! how unhappy is every sinner who deserteth Thee, the channel of life, and seeketh Thee, not in Thyself, but in that which in itself is nothing, and would have remained nothing hadst Thou not called it out of nothingness! How demented is he who seeketh

[1] *Per aversionem et conversionem.*

Thee, who art Goodness, and, while seeking
Thee, withdraweth from Thee, and turneth
aside his eyes! All seekers seek only the good,
and every seeker after the good who withdraweth from Thee withdraweth from that
he seeketh.

Every sinner, then, strayeth from Thee and
departeth afar off. Yet so soon as he return
unto Thee Thou dost hasten to meet him, and
before he perceiveth Thee, Thou dost cast
Thine eyes of mercy on him, with fatherly
love. For with Thee 'tis one to behold and to
pity. Accordingly, Thy mercy followeth every
man so long as he liveth, whithersoever he
goeth, even as Thy glance never quitteth any.
So long as a man liveth, Thou ceasest not to
follow him, and with sweet and inward warn-
ing to stir him up to depart from error and to
turn unto Thee that he may live in bliss.

Thou, Lord, art the companion of my pil-
grimage; wheresoever I go Thine eyes are
alway upon me. Now with Thee seeing is
motion. Therefore Thou movest with me and
never ceasest from motion so long as I move.
If I am at rest, there Thou art with me also.
If I ascend, Thou ascendest, if I descend,
Thou descendest; whithersoever I turn me,
there Thou art. Nor dost Thou desert me in

the day of trouble; as often as I call upon
Thee, Thou art near. For to call upon Thee
is to turn unto Thee, and Thou canst not fail
him that turneth unto Thee, nor could any turn
unto Thee wert not Thou already at hand.
Thou art present before I turn unto Thee.
For, unless Thou wert present and didst entreat
me, I should know naught at all of Thee, and
how could I turn unto Thee whom I knew
not at all?

Thou, then, my God, art He who beholdeth
all things. And with Thee to behold is to work.
So Thou workest all things. Therefore not
unto us, O Lord, not unto us, but unto Thy
great Name, which is Θεός, I will sing glory
for ever. For I have naught save that Thou
givest, nor could I keep that Thou hast given
didst not Thou Thyself preserve it. Thus Thou
ministerest all things unto me. Thou art the
Lord, powerful and pitiful, who givest all;
Thou art the Minister who administerest all;
Thou art the Provider, and He that taketh
thought for us, and our Preserver. And all
these things Thou workest with one simplest
glance of Thine, Thou who art blessed for
evermore.

CHAPTER VI

Of seeing Face to Face

O Lord my God, the longer I look upon Thy
face the more keenly dost Thou seem to turn
the glance of Thine eyes upon me! Thy gaze
causeth me to consider how this image of Thy
face is thus perceptibly painted, since a face
cannot be painted without colour, nor can
colour exist without quantity. But I perceive,
not with my fleshly eyes, which look on this
icon. of Thee, but with the eyes of my mind
and understanding, the invisible truth of Thy
face, which therein is signified, under a shadow
and limitation. Thy true face is freed from any
limitation, it hath neither quantity nor quality,
nor is it of time or place, for it is the Absolute
Form, the Face of faces.

When, therefore, I meditate on how that
face is truth, and the most adequate measure
of all faces, I am brought into a state of great
wonder. For that face which is the true type
of all faces hath not quantity. Wherefore, it is
neither greater nor less than others, and yet
'tis not equal to any other; since it hath not

quantity, but 'tis absolute, and exalted above all. It is, therefore, the Truth, which is equality, freed from all quantity. Thus, then, Lord, I comprehend Thy face to precede every face that may be formed, and to be the pattern and true type of all faces, and all faces to be images of Thy face, which may not be limited or shared. Each face, then, that can look upon Thy face beholdeth naught other or differing from itself, because it beholdeth its own true type. And the pattern truth cannot be other or differing, but those attributes are found in the image just by reason that it is not the very pattern.

Thus, then, while I look on this pictured face, whether from the east or from the west or south, it seemeth in like manner itself to look on me, and, after the same fashion, according as I move my face, that face seemeth turned toward me. Even so is Thy face turned toward all faces that look upon Thee. Thy glance, Lord, is Thy face. He, then, who looketh on Thee with loving face will find Thy face looking on himself with love, and the more he shall study to look on Thee with greater love, by so much shall he find Thy face more loving. He who looketh on Thee in wrath shall in like manner find Thy face wrathful. He who

looketh on Thee with joy shall find Thy face
joyful, after the same sort as is his own who
looketh on Thee. 'Tis as when the eye of flesh,
looking through a red glass, thinketh that it
seeth all things red, or, looking through a
green glass, all things green. Even so the eye
of the mind, muffled up [1] in limitation and
passivity, judgeth Thee, the mind's object,
according unto the nature of its limitation and
passivity.

Man can only judge with human judgment.
When a man attributeth a face unto Thee, he
doth not seek it beyond the human species,
because his judgment, bound up with human
nature, in judging transcendeth not its limitation and passivity.   In like manner, if a lion
were to attribute a face unto Thee, he would
think of it as a lion's; an ox, as an ox's, and
an eagle, as an eagle's.

O Lord, how marvellous is Thy face,
which a young man, if he strove to imagine
it, would conceive as a youth's; a full-grown
man, as manly; an aged man, as an aged
man's! Who could imagine this sole pattern,
most true and most adequate, of all faces—of
all even as of each—this pattern so very perfectly of each as if it were of none other? He

[1] Randall's happy rendering of *obvolutus*.

would need to go beyond all forms of faces
that may be formed, and all figures. And how
could he imagine a face when he must go
beyond all faces, and all likenesses and figures
of all faces, and all concepts which can be
formed of a face, and all colour, adornment,
and beauty of all faces? Wherefore he that
goeth forward to behold Thy face, so long as
he formeth any concept thereof, is far from
Thy face. For all concept of a face falleth short,
Lord, of Thy face, and all beauty which can
be conceived is less than the beauty of Thy
face; every face hath beauty yet none is
beauty's self, but Thy face, Lord, hath beauty
and this having is being. 'Tis therefore Absolute Beauty itself, which is the form that giveth
being to every beautiful form. O face exceeding
comely, whose beauty all things to whom it is
granted to behold it, suffice not to admire!

In all faces is seen the Face of faces, veiled,
and in a riddle[1]; howbeit unveiled it is not
seen, until above all faces a man enter into a
certain secret and mystic silence where there is
no knowledge or concept of a face. This mist,
cloud, darkness or ignorance into which he
that seeketh Thy face entereth when he goeth
beyond all knowledge or concept, is the state

[1] Cf. p. 17, note 1.

below which Thy face cannot be found except
veiled; but that very darkness revealeth Thy
face to be there, beyond all veils. 'Tis as when
our eye seeketh to look on the light of the sun
which is its face; first it beholdeth it veiled in
the stars, and in colours and in all things that
share its light. But when it striveth to behold
the light unveiled, it goeth beyond all visible
light, because all this is less than that which
it seeketh. A man seeking to see a light beyond
his seeing knoweth that, so long as he seeth
aught, it is not that which he seeketh. Wherefore it behoveth him to go beyond all visible
light. For him, then, who must go beyond all
light, the place he entereth must needs lack
visible light, and is thus, so to speak, darkness
to the eye. And while he is in that darkness
which is a mist, if he then know himself to be
in a mist, he knoweth that he hath drawn
nigh the face of the sun; for that mist in his
eye proceedeth from the exceeding bright
shining of the sun. Wherefore, the denser he
knoweth the mist to be, by so much the more
truly doth he attain in the mist unto the light
invisible. I perceive that 'tis thus and not
otherwise, Lord, that the light inaccessible,
the beauty and radiance of Thy face, may,
unveiled, be approached.

CHAPTER VII

What is the Fruit of seeing Face to Face
and how it is to be had

So sweet is the food wherewith Thou, Lord, dost now nourish my soul that it helpeth itself as best it may by all experiences of this world as well as by those most acceptable comparisons which Thou inspirest. For Thou art, Lord, that power or principle from which come all things, and Thy face is that power and principle from which all faces are what they are; and, this being so, I turn me to this nut-tree —a big, tall tree—and seek to perceive its principle. I see it with the eye of sense to be big and spreading, coloured, laden with branches, leaves, and nuts. Then I perceive with the eye of the mind that that tree existed in its seed, not as I now behold it, but potentially. I consider with care the marvellous might of that seed, wherein the entire tree, and all its nuts, and all the generative power of the nuts, and all trees, existed in the generative power of the nuts. And I perceive how that power can never be fully explicated in any time measured by the motion of the heavens, yet how that same power, though beyond explication, is still limited, because it availeth only in this particular species of nuts. Wherefore, albeit in the seed I perceive the tree, 'tis yet in a limited power only. Then, Lord, I consider how the generative power of all the divers species of trees is limited each to its own species, and in those same seeds I perceive the virtual trees.

If, therefore, I am fain to behold the Absolute Power of all such generative powers— which is the power, and likewise the principle, giving power to all seeds—I must needs pass beyond all generative power which can be known or imagined and enter into that ignorance wherein no vestige whatsoever remaineth of generative power or energy. Then in the darkness I find a Power most stupendous, not to be approached by any power imaginable, and this is the 'principle, which giveth being to all generative, and other power. This Power, being absolute, and exalted above all, giveth to every generative power that power wherein it enfoldeth the virtual tree, together with all things necessary to an actual tree and that inhere in the being of a tree; wherefore this principle and cause containeth in itself, as cause, alike enfolded and absolutely, whatso-

ever it giveth to its effect. Thus I perceive this
Power to be the countenance or pattern of all
tree countenances and of every tree; whence
I behold in it that nut-tree, not as in its limited
generative power, but as in the cause and
creating energy of that generative power.
Accordingly, I see that tree as a certain explication of generative power, and the seed as
a certain explication of almighty Power.

I further perceive that—just as in the seed
the tree is not a tree but generative power,
and the generative power is that wherefrom
the tree is unfolded, so that naught is to be
found in the tree which doth not proceed
from the generative power—even so the generative power in its cause, which is the Power of
powers, is not generative power but Absolute
Power. And even so, my God, the tree is in
Thee (Thou art Thyself my God), and in Thee
is its own truth and exemplar. In like manner
also, in Thee the seed of the tree is the truth
and exemplar of its own self and of tree and
seed. Thou, God, art Truth and Exemplar.
That limited generative power is that of the
natural species, which is limited to that species,
and existeth therein as a limited principle.
But Thou, my God, art Absolute Power and,
by reason of this, the Nature of all natures.

O God, whither hast Thou led me that I
may perceive Thine Absolute Face to be the
natural face of all nature, to be the face which
is the Absolute Being of all being, to be art,
and the knowledge of all that may be known?
He, then, who meriteth to behold Thy Face
seeth all things openly, and naught remaineth
hidden from him: he who hath Thee, Lord,
knoweth all things and hath all things: he hath
all things who seeth Thee. For none seeth
Thee except he have Thee. None can attain
unto Thee, since Thou art unapproachable:
none, therefore, can possess himself of Thee
except Thou give Thyself to him. How can
I have Thee, Lord, who am not worthy to
appear in Thy sight? How reacheth my prayer
unto Thee since Thou art not to be approached
by any means? How shall I entreat Thee?
For what were more foolish than to entreat
that Thou shouldest give Thyself to me when
Thou art All in all? And how wilt Thou give
Thyself to me if Thou do not with Thyself
give me heaven and earth and all that in
them are? Nay more, how wilt Thou give me
Thyself if Thou hast not given me mine own
self also? [1]

[1] Cf. St. Bernard: "Ubi se mihi dedit me mihi reddidit"
(quoted by C. E. Rolt, *Dionysius the Areopagite*, p. 165, note 1.)

When I thus rest in the silence of contemplation, Thou, Lord, makest reply within my heart, saying: Be thou thine and I too will be thine.—O Lord, Thou Sweetness most delectable, Thou hast left me free to be mine own self, if I desire. Hence, if I be not mine own self, Thou art not mine, for Thou dost make freewill needful,[1] since Thou canst not be mine if I be not mine own. Since Thou hast thus left me free, Thou dost not constrain me, but Thou awaitest that I should choose to be mine own. This resteth, then, with me, and not with Thee, Lord, who dost not limit Thy supreme lovingkindness, but dost pour it out most abundantly on all able to receive it. Thou, Lord, art Thyself Thy lovingkindness. But how shall I be mine own unless Thou, Lord, shalt teach me? Thou teachest me that sense should obey reason and that reason should bear sway. I am, then, mine own when sense serveth reason: but reason hath not whence it may be guided save by Thee, Lord, who art the Word, and the Reason of reasons. Whence I now perceive that, if I hearken unto Thy Word, which ceaseth not to speak within me, and continually enlighteneth my reason, I shall be mine

---

[1] Reading *necessitas* for *necessitates* in the text.

own, free, and not the slave of sin, and Thou wilt be mine, and wilt grant me to behold Thy face, and then I shall be whole.

Blessed, then, be Thou in Thy gifts, O God, who alone art able to strengthen my soul, and to raise it up that it may hope to attain unto Thee and to enjoy Thee as its very own gift, and the infinite treasury of all things desirable.

CHAPTER VIII

THAT THE GAZE OF GOD IS ITSELF THE LOVING, EFFECTING, READING, AND POSSESSING OF ALL THINGS IN ITSELF

My heart is not at rest, Lord, because Thy love hath inflamed it with so great desire that it can only rest in Thee. I began to pray the Lord's Prayer, and Thou didst inspire me to consider in what manner Thou art our Father. For Thy love is Thy regard, Thy fatherhood is Thy regard, which embraceth us all in fatherly wise: for we say: Our Father. For Thou art the Father of the whole world, and of each individual. Each saith Our Father, and because of it Thy fatherly love comprehendeth each and all of Thy sons. For a father so loveth all his sons as he doth each one, because he is as much the father of all as he is of each one. He so loveth each of his sons that each may imagine himself to be favoured beyond all.

If, then, Thou art a Father, and our Father, we are Thy sons. But paternal love precedeth

34

filial. As long as we Thy sons look upon Thee
as do sons, Thou ceasest not to look upon us
as doth a father. Therefore Thou wilt be our
fatherly Providence, having fatherly care for
us. Thy regard is providence. But if we Thy
sons reject Thee our Father, we cease to be
Thy sons, nor are we thenceforth free sons nor
our own masters; but, separating ourselves
from Thee, we go into a far country, and then
endure grievous slavery under a prince that is
Thine adversary, O God. But Thou our Father,
who hast granted us freedom because we are
Thy sons and Thou art very Liberty, dost
permit us to depart, and to squander our
liberty and our noblest substance, after the
corrupt desires of our senses. Yet for all that
Thou dost not leave us utterly, but art ever
at our side beseeching us, and Thou speakest
within us, calling us back to return unto Thee,
ever ready to behold us again with Thy fatherly
eye as aforetime, if we return, if we turn again
unto Thee. O pitiful God, look on me, who,
remorseful, now return from my wretched
slavery, from the slime and filth of the swine,
where I perished with hunger, and in Thy
house would seek to be fed after any wise.
Feed me with Thy gaze, O Lord, and teach
me how Thy gaze regardeth every sight that

seeth, and all that may be seen, and each act
of seeing, and every power of seeing, or of being
seen, and all the seeing which thence resulteth.
For with Thee to see is to cause; Thou seest
all things who causest all things.

Teach me, O Lord, how at one glance Thou
discernest both all together and each in particular. When I open a book to read, I see the
whole page confusedly, and, if I wish to distinguish separate letters, syllables, and words,
I must needs turn my particular attention to
each individual thing in succession. I can only
read one letter in turn after another, and one
word after another, and one passage after
another. But Thou, Lord, dost see and read
the whole page together, in an instant. If two
of us read the same thing, one more quickly,
the other more slowly, Thou readest with us
both, and dost appear to read in time, since
Thou readest with them that read; yet dost
Thou see and read it all together, above
and beyond time. For with Thee to see is
to read. Thou from eternity hast seen and
read, together and once and for all, all
written books, and those that can be written,
regardless of time; and, in addition, Thou dost
read those same books one after another with
all who read them. Nor dost Thou read one

thing in eternity and another with them that read in time, but the same; Thou behavest Thyself in the same way, since Thou changest not, being a fixed eternity. Yet eternity, because it is bound up with time, seemeth to be moved with time, albeit motion in eternity is rest.

Lord, Thou seest and hast eyes. Thou art an Eye, since with Thee having is being, wherefore in Thyself Thou dost observe all things. If in me my seeing were an eye, as 'tis in Thee, my God, then in myself I should see all things, since the eye is like a mirror. And a mirror, however small it be, beholdeth in itself the image of a great mountain, and of all that existeth on the surface of that mountain, and so the species of all things are contained in the mirror of the eye. Notwithstanding this, our sight, through the mirror of the eye, can only see that particular object toward which it is turned, because its power can only be determined in a particular manner by the object, so that it seeth not all things contained in the mirror of the eye. But Thy sight, being an eye or living mirror, seeth all things in itself. Nay more, because it is the cause of all things visible, it embraceth and seeth all things in the cause and reason of all, that is, in itself.

Thine eye, Lord, reacheth to all things without turning. When our eye turneth itself toward an object 'tis because our sight seeth but through a finite angle. But the angle of Thine eye, O God, is not limited, but is infinite, being the angle of a circle, nay, of an infinite sphere also, since Thy sight is an eye of sphericity and of infinite perfection. Wherefore it seeth at one and the same time all things around and above and below.

O how marvellous is Thy glance, my God, which is Θεός unto all that examine it! How fair and lovely is it unto all that love Thee! How dread is it unto all them that have abandoned Thee, O Lord my God! For 'tis with Thy glance, Lord, that Thou quickenest every spirit, and makest glad every saint, and puttest to flight every sorrow. Look then on me in mercy, and my soul is healed!

CHAPTER IX

How the Gaze of God is alike Universal and Particular, and what is the Way thereunto

I marvel, Lord, seeing that Thou beholdest at once all men and each individual, even as this painted image whereon I look showeth forth, how the universal coincideth with the particular in Thy faculty of sight? But on consideration I find that my imagination doth not comprehend how this may be, because I seek to judge Thy vision from mine own faculty of sight. Now, Thine is not limited as is mine unto the organ of sight, 'tis thus my judgment is deceived. Thy vision, Lord, is Thine essence.

If I consider human nature, which is simple and one in all men, I find it in each and in all. And, although in itself it be neither eastern nor western, nor southern nor northern, yet it is in the east in dwellers in the east, and

39

in dwellers in the west, in the west. Thus, albeit neither motion nor rest is of the essence of human nature, yet 'tis moved when men move and resteth when they rest, and standeth when they stand. And this at one and the same time, because human nature doth not desert men whether they be moved, or be not moved, whether they sleep, or rest. If this human nature, which is individuated,[1] and is not found outside men, is such that 'tis not more present in one man than in another, and is as perfectly present in one as if it were present in no other, much more highly shall it be so with that unindividuated humanity [2] which is the exemplar [3] and idea of the individuated, and, as it were, its form and truth. For it can never be dissociated from individuated human beings, since it is the form which giveth being to the formal nature of man. No specific form can exist without it, since none of itself hath being, but being cometh from that which existeth of itself, before which there is none other. That form, then, which giveth being unto the species is Absolute Form, and Thou art It, O God, who formest the sky and the earth and all things.

[1] *contracta.*
[2] Or, humanity in general.
[3] Or, pattern.

When, therefore, I consider limited human nature, and through that the Absolute, —seeing, to wit, the Absolute in the limited, like the cause in the effect, and the truth and exemplar in the image—then Thou appearest unto me, my God, as the Exemplar of all men, and as Man of himself, that is, Absolute. And when in like manner I turn me in all species unto the Form of forms, in all these Thou appearest unto me their Idea and Exemplar. Being the Absolute Exemplar, and the most simple, Thou art not composite of several exemplars, but Thou art the one Exemplar, most simple, and infinite, in such wise that Thou art the truest and most adequate Exemplar of all things which can be formed, and of each of them. Thou art, therefore, the Essence of essences, giving power to limited essences to be that which they are.

Apart from Thee, Lord, naught can exist. If, then, Thine essence pervade all things, so also doth Thy sight, which is Thine essence. For even as no created thing can escape from its own proper essence, so neither can it from Thine essence, which giveth essential being to all beings. Wherefore, neither can it from Thy sight. Accordingly, Thou, Lord, seest all things and each thing at one and the same time, and

movest with all that move, and standest with
them that stand. And because there be some
that move while others stand, Thou, Lord,
dost stand and move at the same time, at the
same time Thou dost proceed and rest. For if
both motion and rest be individuated at the
same time in divers beings, and if naught can
exist apart from Thee, and no motion be apart
from Thee, nor any rest; then Thou, Lord, art
wholly present to all these things, and to each,
at one and the same time. And yet Thou
dost not move nor rest, since Thou art exalted
above all, and freed from all that can be conceived or named. Wherefore, Thou standest
and proceedest, and yet at the same time dost
not stand or proceed, and that this painted
face showeth me. For, if I move, its glance
seemeth to move because it quitteth me not;
if, while I am moving, another look on the face
while standing still, its glance in like manner
quitteth not him, but standeth still as he doth.
Howbeit, the condition of motion or standing
cannot rightly suit with a face that is freed from
such conditions, for it is above all standing or
motion, in simplest and absolute infinity; and
'tis on the hither side of this infinity that are
found motion, and rest, and their opposition,
and whatever may be uttered or conceived.

·Hence I observe how needful it is for me to enter into the darkness, and to admit the coincidence of opposites, beyond all the grasp of reason, and there to seek the truth where impossibility meeteth me. And beyond that, beyond even the highest ascent of intellect, when I shall have attained unto that which is unknown to every intellect, and which every intellect judgeth to be most far removed from truth, there, my God, art Thou, who art Absolute Necessity.[1] And the more that dark impossibility is recognised as dark and impossible, the more truly doth His Necessity shine forth, and is more unveiledly present, and draweth nigh.

Wherefore I give Thee thanks, my God, because Thou makest plain to me that there is none other way of approaching Thee than that which to all men, even the most learned philosophers, seemeth utterly inaccessible and impossible. For Thou hast shown me that Thou canst not be seen elsewhere than where impossibility meeteth and faceth me. Thou hast inspired me, Lord, who art the Food of the strong, to do violence to myself, because impossibility coincideth with necessity, and I

[1] *Necessitas*, i.e. a Being that cannot but exist. Necessary existence (or self-existence, or uncaused existence) is identified by many scholastics with the essence of God.

have learnt that the place wherein Thou art
found unveiled is girt round with the coincidence of contradictories,[1] and this is the wall
of Paradise wherein Thou dost abide. The door
whereof is guarded by the most proud spirit
of Reason, and, unless he be vanquished, the
way in will not lie open. Thus 'tis beyond the
coincidence of contradictories that Thou mayest
be seen, and nowhere this side thereof. If, then,
in Thy sight, Lord, impossibility be necessity,
there is naught that Thy sight seeth not.

[1] *contradictoria*. Perhaps "antitheses." This is a favourite
theme with Nicholas, one of the cornerstones of his teaching.

CHAPTER X

How God is seen beyond the Coincidence of Contradictories and how Seeing is Being

I stand before this image of Thy face, my God, and while I look upon it with the eyes of sense, I strive with my inner eyes to behold the truth which is figured forth in this picture, and it seemeth to me, Lord, that Thy glance speaketh. For with Thee speech and sight are one, since in reality they are not different in Thee, who art Very Absolute Simplicity. Thence I prove clearly that Thou seest at the same time all things and each thing.

When I preach, I speak alike and at the same time to the whole congregation in church, and to the individuals present in church; I preach one sermon only, and in that one sermon I speak to individuals. And what the church is to me that, Lord, the whole world is to Thee, with the individual creatures which exist or can exist. Then, if Thou speakest to individuals, Thou seest those things to which

Thou speakest. Thou, Lord, who art the sovran comfort of them that hope in Thee,
inspirest me to praise Thee from myself. For
Thou hast given me a face according as Thou
didst will, and it is seen by all to whom I
preach, individually and at the same time.
Thus my one face is seen by individuals, and
my one speech is wholly heard by individuals.
I, however, cannot separately hear all who
speak together, but I must hear one after another; nor can I separately see all at once,
but one after another. But if such a faculty
were in me as that to be heard were one with
hearing, and to be seen with seeing, and in
like manner to speak with hearing (even as it
is with Thee, Lord, who art the sovran Power),
then indeed I could hear and see all and each
at one and the same time. And just as I could
speak to individuals simultaneously, so, in the
same instant in which I were speaking, I could
see and hear the answers of all and each.

Whence I begin, Lord, to behold Thee in
the door of the coincidence of opposites, which
the angel guardeth that is set over the entrance
into Paradise. For Thou art there where speech,
sight, hearing, taste, touch, reason, knowledge,
and understanding are the same, and where
seeing is one with being seen, and hearing

with being heard, and tasting with being tasted, and touching with being touched, and speaking with hearing, and creating with speaking.

If I were to see as I am seen I should not be a creature. And if Thou, God, didst not see as Thou art seen Thou wouldest not be God Almighty. Thou art to be seen of all creatures, and Thou seest all; in that Thou seest all, Thou art seen of all; for otherwise creatures could not exist, since they exist by Thy seeing. If they saw not Thee who seest them, they would not receive from Thee being; the being of the creature is Thy seeing and the being seen of Thee alike. Thou speakest by Thy Word to all things that are, and callest into being those that are not : Thou callest them to hear Thee, and when they hear Thee then they are. When Thou speakest Thou speakest unto all, and all things hear Thee to which Thou speakest. Thou speakest to the earth and callest it to human nature, and the earth heareth Thee and by this its hearing man is made. Thou speakest to that which is nothing as though it were something, and Thou callest nothing to be something, and that which is nothing heareth Thee because that which was nothing becometh something.

O infinite Power, Thy concept is Thy speech!
Thou conceivest the heaven, and it existeth as
Thou conceivest it; Thou conceivest the earth,
and it existeth as Thou conceivest it; while
Thou conceivest, Thou dost see and speak and
work, and do all else that can be named.
Marvellous art Thou, my God, Thou conceivest once, Thou speakest once! How, then,
do not all things come into being simultaneously, but many of them successively?
How do such diverse things spring from one
only concept? Thou dost enlighten me while
I am on the threshold of the door, showing
me that Thy concept is pure and simple
eternity itself. 'Tis impossible that aught should
be made after eternity pure and simple. For
infinite duration, which is eternity's self, includeth all succession, and all which seemeth
to us to be in succession existeth not posterior
to Thy concept, which is eternity. For Thy
one and only concept, which is also Thy Word,
enfoldeth all and each, while Thine eternal
Word cannot be manifold, nor diverse, nor
changeable, nor mutable, because it is simple
eternity.

Thus, Lord, I perceive that naught existeth
posterior to Thy concept, but that all things
exist because Thou dost conceive them. Thou

conceivest in eternity, but in eternity succession is without succession, 'tis eternity's self, 'tis Thy very Word, O Lord God. Thou hast no sooner conceived aught that appeareth to us in time than it is. For in eternity in which Thou conceivest, all succession in time coincideth in the same NOW of eternity. There is no past nor future where future and past are one with present. The reason why things in this world exist as earlier and later is that Thou didst not earlier conceive such things to exist: hadst Thou earlier conceived them they would have existed earlier. But he in whose thought earlier and later can occur, in such a way that he conceives one thing first and then another, is not almighty. Thus, because Thou art God Almighty, Thou dwellest within the wall of Paradise, and this wall is that coincidence where later is one with earlier, where the end is one with the beginning, where Alpha and Omega are the same.

So then, things alway exist because Thou biddest them exist, and they do not exist earlier because Thou dost not bid them earlier. When I read that Adam existed so many years ago, and that to-day such an one is born, it seemeth impossible that Adam existed then because Thou didst then will it, and likewise that the other is born to-day because Thou hast now willed it, and that nevertheless Thou didst not earlier will Adam to exist than the one born to-day. But that which seemeth impossible is necessity itself, for NOW and THEN are posterior to Thy Word. This is why for him that approacheth Thee, they meet in the wall surrounding the place where Thou abidest in coincidence. For NOW and THEN coincide in the circle of the wall of Paradise. But, O my God, the Absolute and Eternal, it is beyond the Present and the Past that Thou dost exist and utter speech!

CHAPTER XI

How in God is seen Succession without Succession

I EXPERIENCE Thy goodness, my God, which not only doth not contemn me, a miserable sinner, but doth sweetly feed me with a certain desire. Thou hast suggested to me an acceptable comparison touching the unity of Thy mental word or concept, and its variation in things seen in succession. The simple concept of a most perfect clock leads me on so that I become the more delectably rapt in the vision of Thy concept and word. For the simple concept of a clock enfoldeth all succession in time. Suppose, then, a clock to be a concept: though we hear the striking of the sixth hour before the seventh, yet the seventh is only heard when the concept biddeth. Neither is the sixth hour earlier in the concept than the seventh or eighth, but in the one simple concept of the clock no hour is earlier or later than another, although the clock never striketh the hour save when the concept biddeth. 'Tis true to say,

when we hear six o'clock strike, that the sixth
hour striketh then because the concept of the
master so willeth. Since in the thought of God
the clock is a concept, 'tis perceived in some
degree how that which is succession in the
clock existeth without succession in the word
or concept, and how in this simplest concept
are enfolded all motions and sounds and whatsoever we find in succession. Naught of that
which appeareth in succession departeth in any
way from the concept, but 'tis the unfolding of
the concept, seeing that the concept giveth
being to each: naught in consequence hath
existed earlier than it appeared, because it was
not earlier conceived that it should exist. Let
then the concept of the clock represent eternity's self; then motion in the clock repre-
senteth succession. Eternity, therefore, both
enfoldeth and unfoldeth [1] succession, since the
concept of the clock, which is eternity, doth
alike enfold and unfold all things.

Blessed be Thou, O Lord my God, who dost
feed and nourish me with the milk of comparisons; until Thou shalt give me more solid
food, lead me, Lord God, by these paths unto
Thee! For if Thou lead me not, I cannot con-
tinue in the way, by reason of the frailty of

[1] *Complicat . . . explicat* ; and so elsewhere.

my corruptible nature, and of the earthen
vessel that I bear about with me. Trusting in
Thine aid, Lord, I return again to find Thee
beyond the wall of the coincidence of enfolding
and unfolding, and as I go in and go out by
this door of Thy word and Thy concept, I
find sweetest nourishment. When I find Thee
as the power that unfoldeth, I go out: when
I find Thee as the power that alike enfoldeth
and unfoldeth, I go in and go out alike. I go
in, passing from the creatures to Thee, their
Creator, from effects to the Cause; I go out,
passing from Thee, the Creator, to the creature,
from Cause to effects. I go in and go out simultaneously when I perceive how going out is
one with going in, and going in with going out.
In this manner one that reckoneth doth alike
enfold and unfold, for he unfoldeth the power
of unity, and enfoldeth number in unity. For
the creature, to go forth from Thee is to enter
into the creature, and to unfold is to enfold.
When I behold Thee, my God, in Paradise,
girt by that wall of the coincidence of opposites,
I see that Thou dost neither enfold nor unfold,
whether separately or together. For disjunc-
tion and conjunction alike are that wall of
coincidence, beyond which Thou existest, set
free from all that can be spoken or thought.

CHAPTER XII

THAT WHERE THE INVISIBLE IS SEEN THE UNCREATED IS CREATED

THOU hast at times appeared unto me, Lord, as One not to be seen of any creature, because Thou art a God hidden, infinite. Now infinity is beyond all comprehension. Then Thou hast after appeared unto me as One to be seen of all, since a thing existeth in the measure where-in Thou dost behold it, and it could not exist in reality did it not behold Thee: for sight affordeth being, since it is Thine essence. Thus my God, Thou art at once invisible and visible. Thou art invisible in regard to Thine own Being, but visible in regard to that of the creature, which only existeth in the measure wherein it beholdeth Thee. Thou, therefore, my invisible God, art seen of all and art seen in all seeing. Thou art seen by every person that seeth, in all that may be seen, and in every act of seeing, invisible as Thou art, and freed from all such conditions, and exalted above all for evermore.

Therefore, Lord, it behoveth me to scale

that wall of invisible vision beyond which
Thou art to be found. Now the wall is at one
and the same time all things and nothing. For
Thou, who seemest to me to be as it were all
things and naught of all things at once, dwellest
within that lofty wall which no genius can
scale in its own power. Thou seemest to me
at times such that I may think Thee to see all
things in Thyself, as in a living mirror, wherein
all things shine forth; yet because with Thee
sight is knowledge, meseemeth Thou dost not
see all in Thee, as in a living mirror, since in
that case Thy knowledge would spring from
the objects. And then again Thou seemest to
me to behold all things in Thyself, as if power
were looking on itself. Even so the generative
power of a tree, if it could behold itself, would
see in itself the potential tree, because the
generative power is virtually the tree. But,
after this, meseemeth that Thou dost not see
Thyself, and all things in Thee, as power. For
the aspect of a tree in its potential state dif-
fereth from that of a tree in actuality. And
then I discover how Thine infinite power surpasseth a mirror or generative power, and the
coincidence of shining and reflection, of cause
and effect alike, and how that Absolute Power
is Absolute Sight, which is very perfection, and

above all modes of seeing: for all modes which
explain the perfection of seeing are, without
mode, Thy sight, which is Thine essence,
my God.

Yet, most pitiful Lord, permit a worthless
work of Thy hands still to speak with Thee.
If with Thee to see is to create, and Thou
seest naught other than Thyself, but art Thyself the object of Thyself (for Thou seest, and
art to be seen, and art Sight)—how then dost
Thou create things other than Thyself—for
Thou wouldst seem to create Thyself even as
Thou seest Thyself? But Thou dost strengthen
me, Life of my spirit! For, although the wall
of absurdity, which is the coincidence of creating with being created, should seem as if it
were impossible, in that creating and being
created are one (for to admit this would seem
to be to affirm that a thing existeth before it
existeth, since when He createth it it existeth,
and yet it existeth not because it is created)
—yet this is no real difficulty, since with Thee
creation and existence are the same. And
creating and being created alike are naught
else than the sharing of Thy Being among all,
that Thou mayest be All in all, and yet mayest
abide freed from all. For to call into [1] being

---

[1] The text has *ab*, an obvious misprint for *ad*.

things which are not is to make Nothing a
sharer in Being: thus, to call is to create,
while to share is to be created. And beyond
this coincidence of creating and being created
art Thou, Absolute and Infinite God, neither
creating nor creatable, albeit all things are
what they are because Thou art.

O height of riches, how beyond understanding art Thou! While I imagine a Creator
creating, I am still on this side the wall of Paradise! While I imagine a Creator as creatable,
I have not yet entered, but I am in the wall.
But when I behold Thee as Absolute Infinity,
to whom is befitting neither the name of
creating Creator nor of creatable Creator—
then indeed I begin to behold Thee unveiled,
and to enter in to the garden of delights! For
Thou art naught such as can be spoken or
imagined, but art infinitely and absolutely
exalted high above all such things. Wherefore,
albeit without Thee naught is made or can
be made, Thou art not a Creator, but infinitely
more than a Creator; unto Thee be praise and
glory through endless ages. Amen.

CHAPTER XIII

THAT GOD IS SEEN TO BE ABSOLUTE INFINITY

O LORD my God, the Helper of them that seek Thee, I behold Thee in the entrance of Paradise, and I know not what I see, for I see naught visible. This alone I know, that I know not what I see, and never can know. And I know not how to name Thee because I know not what Thou art, and did anyone say unto me that Thou wert called by this name or that, by the very fact that he named it, I should know that it was not Thy name. For the wall beyond which I see Thee is the end of all manner of signification in names. If anyone should set forth any concept by which Thou couldst be conceived, I know that that concept is not a concept of Thee, for every concept is ended in the wall of Paradise. And if anyone should set forth any likeness, and say that Thou wert to be imagined as resembling

58

it, I know in like manner that that is no likeness of Thee. So too, if any were to tell of the
understanding of Thee, wishing to supply a
means whereby Thou mightest be understood,
this man is yet far from Thee. For Thou art
separated by an exceeding high wall from all
these. The high wall separates Thee from all
that can possibly be said or thought of Thee,
forasmuch as Thou art Absolute above all the
concepts which any man can frame.

Thus, while I am borne to loftiest heights,
I behold Thee as infinity. By reason of this,
Thou mayest not be attained, or comprehended, or named, or multiplied, or beheld.
He that approacheth Thee must needs ascend
above every limit and end and finite thing.
But how shall he attain unto Thee who art
the End toward whom he striveth, if he must
ascend above the end? He who ascendeth
above the end, doth he not enter in to what
is undefined and confused, and thus, in regard
to the intellect, into ignorance and obscurity,
which pertain to intellectual confusion? It behoveth, then, the intellect to become ignorant
and to abide in darkness if it would fain see
Thee. But what, O my God, is this intellectual
ignorance? Is it not an instructed ignorance[1]?

[1] Cf. Nicholas' work, *De Docta Ignorantia*.

Thou, God, who art infinity, canst only be approached by him whose intellect is in ignorance, to wit, by him who knows himself to be ignorant of Thee.

How can the intellect grasp Thee, who art infinity? The intellect knoweth that it is ignorant, and that Thou canst not be grasped because Thou art infinity. For to understand infinity is to comprehend the incomprehensible. The intellect knoweth that it is ignorant of Thee, because it knoweth Thou canst not be known, unless the unknowable could be known, and the invisible beheld, and the inaccessible attained. Thou, my God, art Very Absolute Infinity, which I perceive to be an end without an end, but I am unable to grasp how without an end an end should be an end. Thou, God, art the End of Thine own self, for Thou art whatever Thou hast; if Thou hast an end, Thou art an End. Thou art therefore an infinite End, because Thou art the End of Thine own self. Since Thine end is Thine essence, the essence of the end is not determined or ended in any place other than the end, but in itself. The end, then, which is its own end, is infinite, and every end which is not its own end is a finite end. Thou, Lord, who art the End ending all things, art the End whereof there is no end, and thus an end without an end, or infinite. This eludeth all reason, because it implieth a contradiction. Thus, when I assert the existence of an end without an end, I admit darkness to be light, ignorance to be knowledge, and the impossible to be a necessity. Since we admit the existence of an end of the finite, we needs must admit the infinite, or the ultimate end, or the end without an end. Now we cannot but admit the existence of finite beings, wherefore we cannot but admit the infinite. Thus we admit the coincidence of contradictories, above which is the infinite.

Howbeit, this coincidence is a contradiction without contradiction, even as an end without an end. And Thou, Lord, sayest unto me that, just as otherness in unity is without otherness because it is unity, even so, in infinity, contradiction is without contradiction, because it is infinity. Infinity is simplicity itself, contradiction existeth not without becoming other. Yet in simplicity otherness existeth without becoming other because it is simplicity itself, seeing that all that is said of absolute simplicity coincideth therewith, because therein having is being. Therein the opposition of opposites is an opposition without opposition, just as the end of things finite is an end without an end. Thou, then, O God, art the Opposition of opposites, because Thou art infinite, and because Thou art infinite Thou art infinity itself. And in infinity the opposition of opposites existeth without opposition.

O Lord my God, Strength of the weak, I see Thee to be infinity itself, wherefore naught is alien to Thee, naught differing from Thee, naught opposed to Thee. For the infinite brooketh not otherness from itself, since, being infinity, naught existeth outside it: absolute infinity includeth and containeth all things. If infinity could ever exist, and aught else exist outside it, then neither infinity nor aught else could exist. Infinity cannot be greater or less; naught, therefore, existeth outside it. Did infinity not include in itself all being, it were not infinity. If it were not infinity, then neither would the finite exist, nor aught alien or different, since these cannot exist without otherness of ends and limits. If the infinite be taken away, naught remaineth. Infinity, accordingly, existeth, and enfoldeth all things, and naught can exist outside it, hence naught is alien to it or differing from it. Thus infinity is alike all things and no one of them all. No name can suit infinity, for every name can

have its contrary, but naught can be contrary
to infinity, which is unnameable. Neither is
infinity a whole, whereunto a part is opposed,
nor can it be a part: 'tis neither great nor
small, nor any of all those things that can be
named in heaven or earth; above all these it
existeth, infinity. Infinity is neither greater nor
less than anything, nor equal thereunto.

But while I consider infinity, how it is neither
greater nor less than any given thing, I declare
it to be the measure of all things, just because
it is neither greater nor less. Thus I conceive
it as equality of being. Yet such equality is
infinity, and therefore it is not equality after
the style in which inequality is opposed to
equality, but therein inequality is equality: for
in infinity inequality existeth without inequality
because it is infinity; so too in infinity equality
is infinity. Infinite equality is an end without
end; whence, albeit it be not greater nor less,
'tis yet not on that account equality in the
manner in which limited equality is understood;
nay, 'tis infinite equality, which admitteth not
greater or less. And so 'tis not more equal to
one thing than to another, but is as equal to
one as to all, and to all as to none. For the
infinite is not liable to limitation, but abideth
absolute: if aught could be limited in infinity,

'twould not be infinite. Hence it may not be limited to equality with the finite, albeit 'tis not unequal to anything. For how could inequality suit with the infinite, when neither greater nor less doth so? The infinite, then, with regard to any given thing, is neither greater, nor less, nor unequal. Nor yet, by reason of this, is it equal to the finite, seeing that, [considered] [1] in itself, it is above all that is finite. The infinite, then, is utterly absolute, and illimitable.

O how exalted art Thou, Lord, above all things, and humble withal, since Thou art in all! If infinity could be limited to anything that can be named, such as a line, or surface, or species, it would draw unto itself that whereto it was limited, and this implieth that the infinite would be limitable, since, though not limited, it would draw unto [itself a limit]. If I should say that the infinite is limited to a line, as when I speak of an infinite line, then the line is drawn unto the infinite, for a line ceaseth to be a line when it hath no quantity nor end. An infinite line is not a line, but a line at infinity is infinity. Just as naught can be added to the infinite, even so the infinite cannot be limited unto anything so as to

[1] [Considered] and [itself a limit] below are not in the Latin.

become aught other than infinite. Infinite goodness is not goodness, but infinity; infinite quantity is not quantity, but infinity, and so with the rest.

Thou art the great God, of whose greatness there is no end, and thus I perceive Thee to be the immeasurable measure of all things, even as the infinite end of all. Wherefore, Lord, being infinite, Thou art without beginning and end; Thou art beginning without beginning and end without end; Thou art beginning without end and end without beginning; Thou art equally beginning as end and end as beginning, yet neither beginning nor end, but above beginning and end, absolute infinity itself, blessed for ever!

CHAPTER XIV

How God enfoldeth all things without Otherness

I SEE, Lord, through Thine infinite mercy, that Thou art infinity encompassing all things. Naught existeth outside Thee, but all things in Thee are not other than Thee. Thou dost teach me, Lord, how otherness, which is not in Thee, is not even in itself, nor can it be. Nor doth otherness, being not in Thee, make one creature to be different from another, albeit one be not another; the sky is not the earth, though 'tis true that sky is sky and earth is earth. If, then, I seek for otherness, which is neither in Thee nor yet outside Thee, where shall I find it? And if it existeth not, how cometh it that the earth is a different creature from the sky? for without otherness this cannot be conceived. But Thou, Lord, dost speak in me and say that there is no positive principle of otherness, and thus it existeth not: for how could otherness exist without a principle, unless it itself were a principle and infinity? Now

otherness cannot be the principle of being,
for otherness taketh its name from not-being,
for because one thing is not another it is called
other. Otherness, therefore, cannot be the
principle of being, because it taketh its name
from not-being, nor hath it the principle of
being, since it ariseth from not-being. Otherness, then, is not anything, but the reason
wherefore the sky is not the earth is because
the sky is not infinity's self, which encom-
passeth all being. Whence, since infinity is
absolute infinity, it resulteth that one thing
cannot be another.

For example, the being of Socrates [1] encom-
passeth all Socratic being, and in Socratic
being pure and simple there is no otherness
nor diversity. The being of Socrates is the
individual unity of all those things that are
in Socrates, in such a way that in that one
being is enfolded the being of all those things
which are in Socrates, to wit, in that individual simplicity wherein naught is found other
or diverse. But in that same single being all
things which have the Socratic being exist and
are unfolded, and outside it they neither exist
nor can exist. Howbeit, in this onefold being,

[1] The name Socrates denotes any man—as usual in the
writings of Scholastics.

when all is said, the eye is not the ear and the head is not the heart, and sight is not hearing, and sense is not reason. Nor doth this result from any principle of otherness, but, granted the Socratic being pure and simple, it resulteth that the head is not the foot because the head is not that most simple Socratic being itself and hence its being doth not contain the whole Socratic being. Thus I perceive—Thou, Lord, enlightening me—that, because Socratic being pure and simple is utterly incommunicable, and not to be limited to the being of any one member—the being of any one member is not the being of any other, but that Socratic being pure and simple is the being of all the members of Socrates, wherein all variety and otherness of being that happeneth in the members is unity pure and simple, even as plurality of forms of parts is unity in the form of the whole.

Thus in some manner, O God, is it with Thy Being, which is absolutely infinity, in relation to all things which exist. But I say absolutely: as the absolute form of being of all limited forms. The hand of Socrates, being separated from Socrates, as after amputation, is no longer the hand of Socrates; yet it still retaineth some kind of being as a corpse. And the reason of this is that the form of Socrates which giveth being doth not give being pure and simple, but a limited being, to wit, the Socratic. From this the being of the hand may be separated, and may yet none the less remain under another form; but if once the hand were separated from the being that is entirely unlimited, to wit, from the infinite and absolute, then it would utterly cease to exist, because it would be cut off from all being.

I give Thee thanks, O Lord my God, who dost bountifully reveal Thyself unto me, in so far as I can receive it, showing how Thou art infinity's self, enfolding the being of all in its most simple power; and this were not infinity were it not infinitely united. For power united is stronger. Accordingly, that power which is united in the highest degree is infinite and almighty. Thou art God Almighty, because Thou art absolute simplicity, which is absolute infinity.

CHAPTER XV

How actual Infinity is Unity, wherein the Figure is Truth

Sustain yet awhile Thy poor little servant that he may speak with Thee, his God! He hath no wit save what Thou grantest him.

I behold in the face of the picture a figure of infinity, for its gaze is not limited to one object or place, and is thus infinite, seeing that it is not more turned to one than to another of them that look upon it. Yet, albeit its gaze is infinite in itself, it seemeth to one regarding it to be limited, since it looketh so fixedly on any beholding it as if it looked on him alone and on naught else. Wherefore Thou appearest unto me, Lord, as a being potentially absolute and infinite, that can be formed and determined by every form. For we say that the determinable potentiality of matter is infinite, seeing that 'tis never utterly exhausted.

But Thou, O infinite Light, makest answer within me that absolute potentiality is infinity itself, which is beyond the wall of coincidence, where potential becoming is one with potential creating, where potentiality is one with act. Matter, although it exist potentially in relation to infinite forms, can yet not possess them in act, but the potentiality is determined by one form, or, if this be removed, by some other. If the potential being of matter were one with the act, it would itself be in the same sense potentiality and act; and just as it was potentiality in relation to infinite forms, so in act it would be infinitely clothed with form. But infinity in act is without otherness, and cannot be infinity unless it be unity. There cannot, then, be an infinite number of forms in act, for actual infinity is unity.

Thou, God, who art Very Infinity, art that one Very God in whom I see all potential being to be actual being. For potency wholly freed from all potentiality limited to matter or to any passive potentiality, is absolute being, for all that existeth in infinite being is itself infinite being pure and simple. Thus, in infinite being, the potential being of all things is infinite being itself. In like manner, in infinity, the actual being of all is infinite being itself. And so in Thee, my God, absolute potential being and absolute actual being could not exist wert Thou not, my God, infinite. My God, Thou art all potential being.

The potential being of matter is material, and thus limited and not absolute; in like manner, the potential being of sense and reason is limited, but that which cannot in any way be limited is one with the Absolute pure and simple, to wit, with infinity. Accordingly, when Thou, my God, appearest unto me as matter that may be formed, in that Thou receivest the form of whosoever looketh on Thee, Thou dost raise me up that I may perceive how he who looketh on Thee doth not give Thee form, but seeth himself in Thee, because from Thee he receiveth that which he is. And so that which Thou appearest to receive from him that looketh on Thee is truly Thy gift to him, Thou being as it were a living mirror of eternity, which is the Form of forms. While any looketh in this mirror, he seeth his own form in the Form of forms, to wit, in the mirror, and he judgeth the form which he seeth in that mirror to be a figure of his own form because 'tis so with a polished material mirror. Yet 'tis the contrary which is true, for in that mirror of eternity what he seeth is not a figure, but the truth, whereof the beholder himself is a figure. Wherefore, in Thee, my God, the figure is the truth, and the exemplar of all things that exist or can exist, and of each of them.

O God, who art marvellous to every mind, at times Thou seemest to be shadow, Thou who art light! While I perceive how the glance of Thine icon seemeth to change in accord with my changing, and Thy face seemeth to be changed—because of this change, Thou appearest to me like the shadow following the movement of one that walketh; but 'tis because I am a living shadow and Thou the truth that I judge from the change of the shadow that the truth changeth also. Wherefore, my God, Thou art alike shadow and truth, Thou art alike the image and exemplar of myself and of all men.

O Lord God, who enlightenest men's hearts, my face is a true face because Thou, who art truth, hast given it unto me. My face is also an image, since 'tis not the truth itself, but an image of absolute truth. Thus in my thought I embrace both truth and the image of my face, and I perceive that therein the image is one with facial truth so that, in the measure it is an image, it is true. Then, Lord, Thou showest me how, in accord with the movement of my face, Thy face is alike moved and un-moved; 'tis moved because it quitteth not the truth of my face, 'tis unmoved, because it followeth not the change of the image. Whence,

even as Thy face quitteth not the truth of my
face, so also it followeth not the movement of
a variable image, for absolute truth is un-
alterable. The truth of my face is changeable,
seeing that it is truth equally with image, while
Thine is unchangeable, seeing that it is image
equally with truth. Absolute truth cannot
abandon the truth of my face, for, did it do
so, my face, being as it is changeable truth,
could no longer subsist. Thus, O God, Thine
infinite goodness maketh Thee seem subject
to mutability, since Thou dost never desert
Thy creatures, which *are* subject to mutability;
howbeit, because Thou art absolute goodness,
Thou art not changeable, inasmuch as Thou
followest not mutability. O the unplumbed
depths of Thee, my God, who dost not abandon
Thy creatures, and followest them not withal!

O Lovingkindness beyond unfolding, Thou
dost offer Thyself to him that beholdeth Thee
as though Thou receivest being from him, and
dost conform Thyself unto him that he may
love Thee the more the more Thou seemest
like unto himself! We cannot hate ourselves,
hence we love that which partaketh of our
being and goeth along with it; we embrace
our likeness, because we are pictured in the
image, and we love ourselves therein. In the

humility of Thine infinite goodness, O God, Thou dost show Thyself as though Thou wert our creature, that thus Thou mayest draw us unto Thee. For Thou dost draw us unto Thee by every possible means whereby a free and rational creature may be drawn. In Thee, God, being created is one with creating, since the image which seemeth to be created by me is the Truth which createth me. So that thus I may at least comprehend how closely I ought to be knit unto Thee, since in Thee being loved is one with loving. For if I ought to love myself in Thee who art my likeness, I am most especially constrained thereto when I see that Thou lovest me as Thy creature and Thine image. How can a father not love a son who is alike father and son? And if he be right loveworthy who is esteemed as a son and known as a father, art not Thou most chiefly so, who art more esteemed than any son, and better known than any father? Thou, my God, hast willed that filial love should be stablished in esteem, and Thou willest to be more esteemed than any son, and to be known more intimately than any father, because Thou art Love, embracing alike filial and paternal affection. Be Thou then blessed for evermore, Thou who art my most sweet Love, my God!

CHAPTER XVI

How that, unless God were Infinite, He would not be the End of Desire

Fire is ever aglow, so likewise is that yearning love which is directed toward Thee, O God, who art the form of all that is desirable, and that truth which in every desire is desired. In that I have begun to taste, of Thy honey-sweet giving, Thy sweetness beyond understanding—which doth by so much the more please me as it appeareth more limitless—I perceive that the reason wherefore Thou, O God, art unknown to all creatures is that they may have in this divine ignorance a greater rest, as in a treasure beyond reckoning, and inexhaustible. For he who findeth a treasure that he knoweth to be utterly beyond reckoning and unlimited is moved by far greater joy than he who findeth one that may be counted, and that is limited. Hence this divine ignorance of Thy greatness is the most desirable nourishment for my intellect, chiefly when I find such a treasure in my field in such manner that the treasure is mine own.

O Fount of riches, Thou willest to be held in my possession, and yet to abide incomprehensible and infinite, because Thou art the treasury of delights whereof no man can desire an end! How should desire covet not-being? For whether the will covet being or not-being, desire itself cannot rest, but is borne on into infinity.

Thou dost come down, Lord, that Thou mayest be comprehended, and yet Thou abidest beyond reckoning, and infinite; and unless Thou didst abide infinite, Thou wouldest not be the end of desire. Wherefore, Thou art infinite that Thou mayest be the end of all desire.

Now, intellectual desire is not turned toward that which can be greater or more desirable. But all on this side infinity may be greater. The end of desire, therefore, is infinite. Thus Thou, O God, art very infinity, for which alone I yearn in every desire, but to the knowledge of which infinity I cannot approach more nearly than that I know it to be infinite. Wherefore, the more I understand that Thou, my God, art not to be understood, by so much the more I attain Thee, because the more I attain the end of my desire. Accordingly I reject as a delusion any idea occurring to me

which seeketh to show Thee as comprehensible.
My yearning, bright with Thee, leadeth me
unto Thee; it spurneth all that is finite and
comprehensible, for in these it cannot rest,
being led by Thee to Thee. And Thou art
beginning without beginning, and end without end. Wherefore my desire is led by the
eternal beginning, from whom it cometh to
be desire, unto the end without end, and He
is infinite. If then, I, a poor little man, could
not be content with Thee, my God, did I know
Thee to be comprehensible, 'tis because I am
led by Thee to Thee, who art incomprehensible
and infinite.

I behold Thee, O Lord my God, in a kind
of mental trance, for if sight be not sated with
seeing, nor the ear with hearing, then much
less is the intellect with understanding. Accordingly, that which sateth the intellect, or that
is the end thereof, is not that which it understandeth; neither can that sate it which it no
whit understandeth, but that alone which it
understandeth by not understanding. For the
intelligible which it knoweth doth not sate
it, nor the intelligible whereof it is utterly
ignorant, but only the intelligible which it
knoweth to be so intelligible that it can
never be fully understood — 'tis this alone

can sate it. Even so a man's insatiable hunger cannot be appeased by partaking of scanty food, or by food that is out of his reach, but only by food that is within his reach, and which, though it be continuously partaken of, can yet never be utterly consumed, since it is such that by eating 'tis not diminished, being infinite.

CHAPTER XVII

How God, unless He were One and Three, could not be perfectly seen

THOU hast shown Thyself unto me, Lord, as in the highest degree loveable, for Thou art infinitely loveable, my God! Hence Thou couldst never be loved by any in the degree that Thou art loveable, save by an infinite lover. Unless there were an infinite lover, Thou wert not infinitely loveable, for Thy loveableness, to wit, the power of being infinitely loved, existeth because there is a power of loving infinitely. And from these two powers ariseth an infinite bond of love, between the infinite lover and the infinitely loveable, and this bond may not be multiplied. Wherefore, Thou, my God, who art Love, art Love that loveth, and Love that is loveable, and Love that is the bond between these twain. I perceive in Thee, my God, love that loveth and love that is loveable; and by the very fact that I perceive in Thee these twain, I perceive the bond between them. And this is naught other than

that which I behold in Thine absolute unity,
wherein I perceive unity that uniteth, unity
that may be united, and the union of those
twain. But whatsoever I perceive in Thee, that
Thou art, my God.

Thou art, then, that infinite love, which
cannot seem to me natural and perfect love
without a lover, and one loveable, and a bond
between them. For how can I conceive an
entirely perfect and natural love without a
lover, one loveable, and the union of both?
For from limited love I learn that 'tis of the
essence of perfect love that love be loving, and
loveable, and the union of both; now that
which is of the essence of a perfect love in
limitation cannot be lacking in absolute love,
whence limited love draweth whatsoever it
hath of perfection. The simpler love is, the
more perfect it is, and Thou, my God, art
love the most entirely perfect and simple. Thus
Thou art the very essence, most perfect, most
simple, most natural, of love. Hence in Thee,
who art love, the lover is not one thing, and
the loveable another, and the bond between
them a third, but they are one and the same,
even Thou Thyself, my God. Since, then, in
Thee the loveable is one with the lover,
and being loved with loving, this bond of

coincidence is an essential bond. For there is
naught in Thee that is not Thy very essence.
Those constituents, then, which appear unto me
to be three, to wit, the lover, the loveable, and
the bond, are that absolute and most simple
essence itself. Thus they are not three, but one.

That Thine essence, my God, which seemeth
to me to be most simple and, so to speak, most
one, is not most natural and most perfect without these three constituents aforenamed. Thus
the essence is triune, and yet there are not three
essences therein, since it is most simple. Wherefore the plurality of these three aforenamed is
alike plurality and unity, and their unity is
alike unity and plurality. Their plurality is
plurality without a plural number, for a plural
number cannot be unity pure and simple,
because it is a plural number. There is no
numerical distinction between the three, for
plural number is essential to distinction, one
number being essentially distinct from another.
And because this unity is triune, 'tis not the
unity of a singular number, for the unity
of a singular number is not triune. O most
wondrous God, Thou art neither of singular
number not yet of plural, but art above all
plurality or singularity, One in Three and
Three in One! I perceive, then, that in

the wall of Paradise, where Thou, my God, dwellest, plurality is one with singularity, and that Thine abode is very far removed beyond them.

Teach me, Lord, how I can conceive that to be possible which I perceive to be necessary! For I am met by the impossibility that the plurality of three elements, without which I cannot conceive Thee as perfect and natural love, should be a plurality without number. When any saith one, one, one, he saith one thrice; he saith not three, but one, and that one thrice. Yet he cannot say it thrice without the number three, although he name not three. When he saith one thrice, he repeateth the same without numbering it, for to number is to make the one other, but to repeat one and the same thing thrice over is to make plural without number. Whence the plurality that I behold in Thee, my God, is an otherness without otherness, because it is an otherness which is identity. For, although I perceive that the lover is not the loveable, and that the bond between them is neither the one nor the other, I do not perceive it in the sense that the lover is one thing and the loveable another; but I perceive that the distinction between lover and loveable is beyond the wall of the coincidence

of unity and otherness. This distinction, which
is beyond the wall where distinguishable and
indistinguishable are one, precedeth all otherness and diversity that can be understood. The
wall is a barrier to the power of every intellect,
albeit the eye penetrate beyond it into Paradise. But what it there seeth it cannot tell nor
understand, for its love is a treasure, secret
and hidden, which, when found, remaineth
hidden, since 'tis found within the wall of
the coincidence of the hidden and the manifest.

But I cannot withdraw me from the sweetness of the vision before that I have in some
manner brought home to myself the revelation
of the distinction between the lover, the loveable, and the bond between them. For one
may, it seemeth, by a figure, win some slight
foretaste of that sweetest food. Thou, Lord,
grantest me to see in Thee love, because I see
myself as lover. And seeing that I love myself
I see myself as loveable, and myself to be the
most natural bond between the twain: I am
lover, I am loveable, I am bond. Accordingly,
that love without which none of these three
constituents could exist, is one. 'Tis the same,
one I who am lover, and who am loveable,
and who am the bond arising from the love
wherewith I love myself: I am one, and not

three. Suppose, then, that my love were my
essence, as 'tis in my God—then in the unity
of my essence there would exist the unity of
the three constituents aforesaid, and in their
trinity, the unity of my essence: all would
exist in limitation in my essence, after the
manner in which I perceive them to exist
truly and absolutely in Thee. Yet the love that
loveth would not be the love that is loveable,
nor the bond between them: this I learn by
the following practice.

The active love which I extend to an object
outside myself, as to something loveable outside
my own essence, is followed by a bond whereby
I am attached to that object, as far as in me
lieth: the object is not attached to me by the
same bond, since perchance it loveth me not.
Whence, albeit I so love it that my active
love overfloweth itself, that active love of
mine doth yet not draw out the love of me
as loveable; for I do not become loveable in
the other's sight, he careth not for me, albeit
I love him much: 'tis as when a son sometimes
careth not for his mother who loveth him most
tenderly. And so I learn by experience that
love that loveth is not love that is loveable,
nor their bond, but I see that the lover is to
be distinguished from the loveable and from

their bond. This distinction, howbeit, is not of the essence of love, since I cannot love either myself or any being other than myself without love : thus love is of the essence of the three. Thus I perceive that the essence of these three constituents aforesaid is entirely onefold, albeit they are distinct one from the other.

I have set forth, Lord, by a comparison some kind of foretaste of Thy nature. Yet in mercy forgive me that I strive to image forth the unimaginable savour of Thy sweetness. If the sweetness of some fruit unknown may not be pictured through any painting or image, or described in any words, who am I, a miserable sinner, who strive to show Thee, that art beyond showing, and to image Thee, the invisible, as visible, and who make bold to render delectable that Thine infinite and all-ineffable sweetness? Never yet have I merited to taste thereof, and the words whereby I set it forth do rather minish than magnify it. But so great is Thy goodness, my God, that Thou permittest even the blind to speak of the light, and to herald the praises of Him of whom they neither know nor can know aught save it be revealed unto them.

Revelation, howbeit, reacheth not unto taste, the ear of faith reacheth not unto the sweetness

of this foretaste. Yet, Lord, Thou hast revealed
unto me that ear hath not heard, nor hath it
entered into the heart of man, that infinity
of Thy sweetness, which Thou hast prepared
for them that love Thee. This Thy great
Apostle Paul revealed unto us, who was rapt,
beyond the wall of coincidence, into Paradise,
where alone Thou mayest be seen unveiled,
O Thou Fount of delights! I have endeavoured
to submit me to be rapt, trusting in Thine
infinite goodness, that I might behold Thee
to be invisible, and the vision revealed to be
beyond revealing. Thou knowest how far I
have come, I know not: but Thy grace is
sufficient for me, whereby Thou assurest me
that Thou art incomprehensible, and dost
uplift me to a firm hope that, with Thee for
guide, I shall come to the fruition of Thee.

CHAPTER XVIII

How God, unless He were a Trinity, could not be Bliss

WOULD, Lord, that all who by Thy gift have received eyes of the mind would open them, and would see with me how Thou art a jealous [1] God! For Thou, Love that lovest, canst hate nothing; for 'tis in Thee, O loveable God, that all things loveable are enfolded, and Thou lovest each of them. They would thus see with me the alliance or bond whereby Thou art united unto all.

Thou lovest, Lord, and lovest alike all in general and each in particular, Thou spreadest Thy love over all. Yet many love not Thee, but prefer something other than Thyself to Thee. If loveable love were not distinct from active love, Thou wouldst be seen so loveable by all that they could not love aught beside

[1] Cf. Dionysius, *De Divinis Nominibus*, iv. 13 (ed. Rolt, p. 106): "Jealous, because He is vehement in His good yearning towards the world."

88

Thee, and all reasoning spirits would be constrained to love Thee. But Thou art so magnanimous, my God, that Thou willest reasoning
spirits to be free to love Thee or not. Wherefore it followeth not on Thy loving that Thou
art loved. Thou therefore, my God, art united
by a bond of love to all, because Thou spreadest
Thy love over every creature of Thine. But
not every reasoning spirit is united unto Thee,
because it directeth its love, not toward Thy
loveableness, but toward some other thing
whereunto it is united and bound. Thou
hast espoused unto Thyself, by Thine active
love, every reasoning soul; but every spouse
loveth not Thee, her Betrothed, but too often
some other unto whom she cleaveth. But how,
my God, could Thy spouse, the human soul,
attain her end if Thou wert not loveable, that
thus, by loving Thee, the loveable, she might
attain to be knit unto Thee, and unto most
blissful union?

Who, then, can deny that Thou, God, art
triune, when he perceiveth that, wert Thou
not Three and One, Thou couldst not be
either a magnanimous, or a natural and perfect God, and that the spirit could not enjoy
free will, nor attain to fruition of Thee and to
its own bliss? 'Tis because Thou art an intellect

that understandeth and an intellect that is understood and again the bond between them, that the created intellect can attain in Thee, its intelligible God, union and bliss. In like manner, 'tis because Thou art loveable love, that the created will, by loving, can attain in Thee, its loveable God, union and bliss. For he that receiveth Thee, O God, Thou light that may be received by the reason, might attain unto so close a union with Thee as that of a son with his father.

I perceive, Lord, by Thine enlightening, that the reasoning nature can only attain union with Thee because Thou art loveable and canst be apprehended. Wherefore, human nature cannot be united unto Thee as a loving God (for in this aspect Thou art not its object), but it can be united unto Thee as its loveable God, since the loveable is the lover's object. Thus in like manner the intelligible is the object of the intellect, and this object we call truth. Wherefore, since Thou, my God, art the truth intelligible, the created intellect can be united unto Thee. And thus I perceive that the reasoning human nature can be united only unto Thy divine and intelligible and loveable nature, and that man, taking hold on Thee, a God that may be received, passeth into a bond which, by reason of its being so closely knit, may be given the name of sonship, since sonship is the most close-knit bond we know.

¬If this bond of union be the closest possible, it will of necessity result that, since Thou, the loveable God, canst not more be loved by man, this bond will attain to the most perfect sonship in that sonship which is perfection, embracing all possible sonships, whereby all sons attain final bliss and perfection. In this most exalted Son, sonship is as art in a master or light in the sun. In the rest, 'tis as art in disciples or light in the stars.

CHAPTER XIX

How Jesus is the Union of God and Man

I RENDER unto Thee thanks unspeakable, O God, light and life of my soul. For I now perceive the faith which, by the teaching of the Apostles, the Catholic Church holdeth, to wit, how Thou, a loving God, dost beget of Thyself a loveable God, and how Thou, the loveable God begotten, art the absolute mediator. For 'tis through Thee that all existeth which doth exist or can exist, since Thou, the loving or willing God, enfoldest them all in Thee, the loveable God. For all that Thou, O God, willest or conceivest is enfolded in Thee, the loveable God. Naught can exist except Thou will it to be. Wherefore all things have their cause or reason for being in Thy loveable concept, and the sole cause of them all is that it so pleaseth Thee; naught pleaseth a lover, as a lover, save the loveable. Thou, O loveable God, art the Son of God the loving Father, since in Thee is all the Father's delight.[1] Thus all creatable being is enfolded in Thee, the loveable God.

[1] *complacentia*. Cf. St. Mark, i. 11. Vulg. *in quo complacui*.

Thou too, O loving God—since from Thee
cometh the loveable God, as a son from a
father—art the Father of all beings by reason
that Thou art God, the loving Father of the
loveable God Thy Son. For Thy concept is a
Son, in whom are all things, and Thine union
and Thy concept is act and operation arising
therefrom — the act and operation wherein
existeth the actuality and unfolding of all
things. As therefore of Thee, the loving God,
there is begotten the loveable God, and this
generation is a concept, even so there proceedeth from Thee, the loving God, and from
Thy concept, the loveable God begotten of
Thee, Thine act and concept, to wit, the bond
knitting together and the God uniting Thee and
Thy concept, even as the act of loving uniteth
in love the lover and the beloved. And this
bond is called Spirit; for spirit is like motion,
proceeding from that which moveth and that
which is moved. Thus motion is the unfolding
of the concept of him that moveth. Wherefore
in Thee, God the Holy Spirit, all things are
unfolded, even as they are conceived in Thee,
God the Son.

I perceive, then—Thou, God, enlightening
me—how all things of God the Father are in
Thee, God the Son, as in His reason, concept,

cause, or exemplar, and how the Son mediateth
all things because He is the reason. For 'tis by
means of reason and wisdom that Thou, God
the Father, workest all things, and the spirit
or motion giveth effect unto the concept of
reason, as we learn from the craftsman who,
by the motive power in his hands, giveth
effect unto the coffer which he hath in his
mind. Thus, my God, I perceive how Thy
Son mediateth the union of all things, that all
may find rest in Thee by the mediation of
Thy Son. And I see that blessed Jesus, Son of
Man, is most closely united unto Thy Son, and
that the son of man could not be united unto
Thee, God the Father, save by mediation of
Thy Son, the absolute mediator.

Who would not be ravished to the highest
in the attentive consideration of these things?
Thou, my God, disclosest unto me, a poor
wretch, this so great secret that I may perceive
that man cannot apprehend Thee, the Father,
save in Thy Son, who may be apprehended
and who is the mediator, and that to apprehend Thee is to be united unto Thee. Man,
then, can be united unto Thee through Thy
Son, who is the means of union; and human
nature most closely knit unto Thee, in whatsoever man it be, cannot be more united unto

the intermediary than it is, for without an
intermediary it cannot be united unto Thee.
Thus it is united in the closest degree unto the
intermediary, yet it doth not become the intermediary: wherefore, albeit it cannot become
the intermediary (since it cannot be united
unto Thee without an intermediary), 'tis yet
so joined unto the absolute intermediary that
naught can mediate between it and Thy Son,
the absolute mediator. For if aught could
mediate between human nature and the absolute mediator, human nature would not then
be united unto Thee in the closest degree.

O good Jesu, I perceive that in Thee human
nature is linked most closely unto God the
Father, by that most exalted union through
which it is linked unto God the Son, the
absolute mediator. Since Thou art Son of Man,
human sonship is in the highest degree united
in Thee, Jesu, unto the divine sonship, so that
Thou art rightly called Son of God and Son
of Man, for in Thee naught mediateth between
those twain. In that absolute sonship, which
is the Son of God, is enfolded all sonship,
and thereunto Thy human sonship, Jesu, is
supremely united. Accordingly, Thy human
sonship subsisteth in the divine, not only as
enfolded therein, but as that which is attracted

in that which attracteth, and that which is
united in that which uniteth, and that which
is substantiated in that which giveth substance.
Thus in Thee, Jesu, there can be no possible
separation between Son of Man and Son of
God. Possibility of separation ariseth from the
fact that an union is not of the closest, but,
where an union is of the closest possible, there
no intermediary can exist. Separation, then,
can have no place where naught can mediate
between the things united. But where that
which is united subsisteth not in that which
uniteth, the union is not the closest possible;
for 'tis a closer union where the united subsisteth in the uniter than where it subsisteth
separately, separation being a withdrawal from
perfect union.

Thus in Thee, my Jesu, I see how the human
sonship whereby Thou art Son of Man subsisteth in the divine sonship whereby Thou
art Son of God, as in the most perfect union
that which is united subsisteth in that which
uniteth. Glory be to Thee, O God, throughout
all ages!

CHAPTER XX

How Jesus is understood to be the Union of the Divine Nature and the Human Nature

THOU showest me, O Light unfailing, that the perfect union whereby human nature is united through my Jesus with Thy divine nature is not in any wise like unto infinite union. The union whereby Thou, God the Father, art united unto God Thy Son is God the Holy Spirit, and thus 'tis an infinite union, seeing that it attaineth unto absolute and essential identity. 'Tis not so when human nature is united unto the divine, for human nature cannot pass over into essential union with the divine, even as the finite cannot be infinitely united unto the infinite, because it would pass into identity with the infinite, and thus would cease to be finite when the infinite were verified in it. Wherefore this union, whereby human nature is united unto the divine nature, is naught else than the attraction in the highest degree of the human nature unto the divine,

in such wise that human nature, as such, could
not be attracted to greater heights. This union,
then, of human nature, as such, with the
divine is the greatest, in the sense of being
the greatest possible, but it is not purely and
simply the greatest, and infinite, as is the
divine union.

Thus through the bounty of Thy grace I
see in Thee, Jesu, Son of Man, the Son of God,
and in the Son of God, the Father. Now, in
Thee the Son of Man I see the Son of God,
because Thou art both of these alike, and in
Thy finite nature which is attracted I perceive
the infinite nature which attracteth; in the
absolute Son I behold the absolute Father, for
the Son cannot be seen as Son unless the
Father be seen. I behold in Thee, Jesu, the
divine sonship which is the truth of all sonship, and equally with it the highest human
sonship, which is the most approximate image
of the absolute sonship. Just as the image,
between which and the exemplar no more
perfect image can be interposed, hath an
existence nearest in truth to the object whereof
it is the image, even so I perceive Thy human
nature subsisting in the divine nature.

Accordingly, I see in Thy human nature all
that I see in the divine, but I see that in Thy

human nature those attributes exist in human
guise which in the divine nature are divine
truth itself. That which I see to exist in human
guise in Thee, Jesu, is a likeness unto the
divine nature, but the likeness is united unto
the exemplar without a medium, in such
wise that no greater likeness can exist or be
imagined. In Thy human or rational nature
I see the rational human spirit most closely
united unto the divine Spirit, which is absolute reason, and so the human intelligence
and all things in Thine intelligence, Jesu,
united unto the divine intelligence. For Thou,
Jesu, as God, dost understand all, and to
understand in this sense is to be all. As
Man, Thou understandest all, and to understand in this sense is to be a likeness of all.
For man only comprehendeth things by a likeness; a stone existeth not in human understanding as in its proper cause or nature, but
as in its specific idea and likeness. Thus in
Thee, Jesu, human intelligence is united unto
the divine intelligence itself, even as a most
perfect image unto the truth of its pattern. If
I consider the ideal form of the coffer in the
craftsman's mind and the species of coffer
made by that master most perfectly carrying
out his idea, I learn how the ideal form is the

truth of the species, and that only in this one master is it united unto it as truth is unto the image. So in Thee, Jesu, Master of masters, I see that the absolute idea of all things, and with it what resembles it in species, are united in the highest degree.

I see Thee, good Jesu, within the wall of Paradise, since Thine intelligence is alike truth and image, and Thou art alike God and creature, alike infinite and finite. And 'tis not possible that Thou shouldst be seen this side of the wall, for Thou art the bond between the divine nature that createth and the human nature that is created.

Howbeit, between Thy human intellect and that of any other man soever I perceive a difference: for no one man knoweth all things that may be known by man, since no man's intellect is so joined unto the exemplar of all things, as the image unto the truth, but that it could not be more nearly joined, and more actually set therein, and so it doth not understand so much but that it could understand yet more, had it access unto the exemplar of things whence every thing actually existent deriveth its actuality. But Thine intellect actually understandeth all that may be apprehended of men, because in Thee human nature is in full perfection, and most entirely joined unto its exemplar. By means of this union, Thy human intelligence exceedeth all created intelligence in perfection of understanding. Wherefore, all rational spirits are far beneath Thee, and Thou, Jesu, art the Master and Light of them all, and Thou art perfection, and the fullness of all things, and by Thee they attain unto absolute truth, as by their mediator. For Thou art alike the way unto truth, and the truth itself; Thou art alike the way unto the life of the intellect and that life itself; Thou art alike the fragrance of the food of joy and the taste that maketh joyful. Be Thou, then, most sweet Jesu, blessed for ever!

CHAPTER XXI

THAT BLISS IS NOT POSSIBLE WITHOUT JESUS

O JESU, Thou end of the universe, in whom
resteth, as in the final degree of perfection,
every creature, Thou art utterly unknown to
the wise of this world. For of Thee we affirm
many antitheses that are yet most true, since
Thou art alike Creator and creature, alike He
that attracteth and He that is attracted, alike
finite and infinite. They pronounce it folly to
believe this possible, and because of it they
flee from Thy Name, and do not receive Thy
light whereby Thou hast illumined 'us. But,
esteeming themselves wise, they remain for
ever foolish, and ignorant, and blind. Yet if
they would believe that Thou art Christ, God
and Man, and would receive and handle the
words of the Gospel as being those of so great
a Master, then at last they would see most
clearly that, in comparison with that light
there hidden in the simplicity of Thy words,
all things else are naught but thickest shadows,

and ignorance. Thus 'tis only humble believers
who attain unto this most gracious and lifegiving revelation. There is hidden in Thy most
holy Gospel, which is heavenly food, as there
was in the manna, sweetness to satisfy all
desire, which can only be tasted by him that
believeth and eateth. If any believeth and
receiveth it, he shall prove and find the truth,
because Thou didst come down from heaven
and Thou alone art the Master of truth.

O good Jesu, Thou art the Tree of Life, in
the Paradise of delights, and none may feed
upon that desirable life save from Thy fruit.
Thou art, O Jesu, the food forbidden to all
sons of Adam who, expelled from Paradise,
seek their sustenance from the earth whereon
they toil. Wherefore it behoveth every man to
put off the old man of presumption and to
put on the new man of humility, which is
after Thy pattern, if he hope to taste the food
of life within the Paradise of delights. The
nature of the new and of the old Adam is one,
but in the old Adam it is animal; in Thee,
the new Adam, it is spiritual, for in Thee,
Jesu, it is united unto God, who is Spirit.
Wherefore, every man must needs be united
in one spirit unto Thee, Jesu, even as he
is by the human nature that is common to

himself and to Thee, to the end that thus in his own nature, which Thou, Jesu, dost share, he may be able to draw near unto God the Father, who is in Paradise. Now to behold God the Father, and Thee, Jesu, His Son, is to be in Paradise, and is glory everlasting. For he that stayeth outside Paradise cannot have such a vision, since neither God the Father nor Thou, Jesu, are to be found outside Paradise.

Every man, then, hath attained bliss who is united unto Thee, Jesu, as a limb unto the head. None can come unto the Father unless he be drawn by the Father. The Father drew Thy humanity, Jesu, by His Son, and by Thee, Jesu, the Father draweth all men. Just as Thy humanity, Jesu, is united unto the Son of God the Father, as unto the means whereby the Father drew it, even so the humanity of every man soever is united unto Thee, Jesu, as unto the one and only means whereby the Father draweth all men. Therefore without Thee, Jesu, 'tis impossible for any man to attain bliss. Thou art, Jesu, the revelation of the Father. For the Father is invisible to all, and visible only to Thee, His Son, and, after Thee, to him who through Thee and Thy revelation shall be found worthy to behold Him. Thou art, therefore, He that uniteth each of the blessed, and each of the blessed subsisteth in Thee, as that which is united in that which uniteth.

None of the wise men of this world can attain true bliss while he knoweth Thee not. None of the blessed can see the Father in Paradise save with Thee, Jesu. Antitheses are made true in the blessed, even as in Thee, Jesu, since he is united unto Thee in a rational, natural and single spirit. For every blissful spirit subsisteth in Thine, as that which is quickened in the lifegiver. Every blissful spirit beholdeth the invisible God and is united in Thee, Jesu, unto God the unapproachable and immortal. And thus in Thee the finite is united unto the infinite, and unto that which is beyond union, and the incomprehensible is possessed in an eternal fruition which is bliss most joyous and inexhaustible. Be merciful unto me, Jesu, be merciful, and grant me to behold Thee unveiled, and my soul is healed!

CHAPTER XXII

How Jesus seeth and how He
hath worked

THE mind's eye cannot be sated in beholding thee, Jesu, because Thou art the fulfilment of all beauty the mind can picture, and in this icon I conjecture Thy right marvellous and astounding [1] sight, Jesu blessed above all. For Thou, Jesu, whilst Thou didst walk this world of sense, didst use eyes of flesh like unto ours. With them Thou didst see, even as we men do, one object and another, for there was in Thine eyes a certain spirit which informed the organ, like the sensitive mind in an animal's body. In that spirit there was a noble power of discernment whereby Thou, Lord, didst see and distinguish between one object of one colour and another of another. And, yet more, from the aspect of the face and eyes of the men whom Thou sawest Thou didst judge truly of the passions of the soul—anger, joy, sorrow. And more subtly still Thou didst

[1] The text has *stupidum*, presumably by misprint for *stupendum*.

106

comprehend from few tokens what was hidden
in a man's mind (for nothing is conceived in
the mind that is not in some way shewn in the
face, which is the heart's herald, and especially in the eyes). By all these tokens Thou
didst much more truly reach the inmost places
of the soul than any created spirit can. From
any one sign, albeit of the slightest, Thou didst
perceive the man's whole thought, even as
understanding men grasp from a few words
an idea that requireth a whole long discourse
to set it forth, and even as the learned, from
running their eye hastily over a book, can
narrate the writer's whole intent as though
they had read it through.

¶ Thou, Jesu, didst excel in this manner of
vision all the perfection, swiftness, and keenness
of all men past, present, and to come, and yet
this sight was human because it was not perfected without the eye of flesh. Howbeit, it
was stupendous and marvellous. For if there
be men who, after prolonged and subtle
examining, can read the mind of a writer,
under characters and signs newly devised at
the time, and unseen before, Thou, Jesu, didst
perceive all things under every sign and figure.

If, as we read, there was once a man who,
by certain tokens in the eye, knew the thoughts

of an interrogator, even the verses that he might be repeating to himself, Thou, Jesu, hadst more skill than all in grasping all the mind's thought from each glance of the eye. I myself have seen a deaf woman who read everything from the movement of her daughter's lips, and understood it as if she had heard it. If such a thing is possible by long practice among deaf and dumb persons, and Religious who converse by signs, Thou, Jesu, who, as a Master of masters, actually knewest all that is to be known, didst more perfectly form a true judgment of the heart and its thoughts from the slightest glances and signs invisible to us.

But unto this Thy human sight, most perfect albeit finite and limited unto an organ, there was united an absolute and infinite sight—the sight whereby Thou, as God, didst see alike all things and each, absent as well as present, past as well as future. Thus, Jesu, with Thy human eye Thou sawest such accidentals as are visible, but, with Thy divine, absolute sight, the substance of things. None save Thee, Jesu, ever in the flesh beheld the substance or essence of things. Thou alone sawest most truly the soul and spirit and whatsoever there was in man. For as in man the faculty of

understanding is linked with the animal faculty
of sight, so that a man not only seeth like an
animal but also, as a man, discerneth and
judgeth, so in Thee, Jesu, the absolute sight
was united unto the human faculty of understanding, which, in the animal sight, is discernment. In man, the faculty of animal sight
subsisteth, not in itself, but in the reasoning
soul, as in the form of the whole: in Thee,
Jesu, the intellectual faculty of sight subsisteth,
not in itself, but in the faculty of absolute
sight. O most sweet Jesu, how marvellous is
Thy sight!

Sometimes it befalleth us to fix our gaze on
a passer-by without giving heed to recognise
who he was; so we cannot tell the name of
that passer-by to any that asketh it, albeit it
is a man we know, and we are aware that
someone hath passed by. We have seen him
as an animal might, not like a man, because
we have not applied our faculty of discernment. Whence we learn that the natures of
our faculties, though they be bound up in one
human form, do yet abide distinct, and have
distinct workings. Even so in Thee, the one
Jesus, I perceive that the human intellectual
nature was united after somewhat the same
fashion unto the divine nature, and that in

like manner Thou didst many works as Man,
and, as God, many marvellous works beyond
what man could do. I see, most loving Jesu,
that the intellectual nature is absolute in regard
to that of the senses, and not, as is the sensible
nature, finite and tied to an organ, as the seeing
faculty of the senses is tied to the eye: but
the divine faculty is immeasurably more absolute, beyond the intellectual. For the human
intellect, if it is to find expression in action,
requireth images,[1] and images cannot be had
without the senses, and senses subsist not without a body; and by reason of this the faculty
of human intelligence is limited, and slight,
requiring the things aforesaid. Now the divine
intelligence is necessity itself, independent, requiring naught — nay, rather do all things
require it, since without it they cannot exist.

I consider more attentively how the discursive [2] faculty which, in the process of
reasoning, runneth hither and thither,[3] and
seeketh, is another thing from the faculty
which judgeth and understandeth. We see a
dog run hither and thither, and seek his
master, and recognise him and hear his call.

[1] *phantasmata.*
[2] Cf. Rolt, *Dionysius the Areopagite*; Discursive *v.* Intuitive
Reason, Introduction, p. 26.
[3] *discurrit.*

This running about is natural to an animal, and in the dog is found in a degree of specific perfection. There are other animals which are even keener in this pursuit,[1] according to their more perfect species, and in man this pursuit most nearly approacheth the intellectual faculty, so that it is the summit of perfection in the senses, embracing many, nay, innumerable degrees of perfection, on a lower level than the intellectual, as the different species of animals reveal unto us. For there is no species which shareth not the degree of perfection proper unto itself. Each of the degrees hath a wide space within whose limits we see individuals of the species partaking of the species in divers ways. In like manner the intellectual nature hath, on a lower level than the divine, innumerable degrees. Whence, just as in the intellectual nature all degrees of perfection of the senses are implied, so in the divine are implied all degrees of perfection, alike of the intellect and of the senses, and all others. Thus in Thee, my Jesu, I behold all perfection.

Since Thou art all-perfect Man, I see in Thee an intellect united unto a rational or discursive faculty, which is the supreme faculty

[1] *discursus*.

of the senses. And thus I see that Thine intellect was set in Thy reason as in its own place, like unto a candle placed in a room, which illumineth the room, and all the walls, and the whole building, howbeit by more or less according to the degree of its distance from them. Finally, I see that in Thee the divine Word is united unto a sovran intellect, and that the place where the Word is received is that intellect itself, just as in ourselves we prove that the intellect is the place where the word of a master is received, as if the sun's light should be joined unto the candle afore chosen. For the Word of God illumineth the intellect as the sun's light illumineth this world. Wherefore in Thee, my Jesu, I perceive the life of the senses illumined by the light of the intellect; the life of the intellect as a light that illumineth and that is illumined; and the divine life, which illumineth alone. For I see in Thine intellectual light the very Fount of light, to wit, the Word of God which is truth, illumining every intellect. Thou only, then, art the highest of all creatures, since Thou art thus at once Creature and blessed Creator.

CHAPTER XXIII

How that when Jesus died His Union
with Life persisted

O Jesu, the mind's most delectable food, when I look upon Thee within the wall of Paradise, how marvellous dost Thou appear unto me! For Thou art the Word of God humanified, and Thou art man deified. Yet art not Thou as it were compounded of God and man. Between component parts some proportion is necessary, without which there can be no composition, but there is no proportion between the finite and infinite. Nor art Thou the coincidence of the creature and Creator, in the sense in which coincidence maketh one thing to be another. For human nature is not divine nor divine nature human. The divine nature is not mutable nor can it be changed into another nature, since it is eternity itself. Nor can any nature by reason of its union with the divine pass over into another nature: as is illustrated in the case of the image, when united unto its truth. For an image cannot be said to become other when thus united, but rather to

withdraw itself from otherness, because it is
united unto its own truth, which is unchange-
ableness itself.

Neither, most sweet Jesu, canst Thou be
said to be of an intermediate nature, between
divine and human, for between these twain it
is not possible for any intermediate nature to
be set, partaking of both. For the divine nature
may not be shared, since it is entirely and
absolutely onefold, nor in that wise wouldst
Thou, blessed Jesu, be either God or man.
But I see Thee, Lord Jesu, to be One Person
beyond all understanding, because Thou art
One Christ, in the same manner that I see
Thy human soul to be one, albeit therein, as
in any human soul, I see there was a nature
of the senses liable to corruption, subsisting in
an intellectual and incorruptible nature.

That soul was not composite of corruptible
and incorruptible, nor is the nature of the
senses one with that of the intellect; but I
perceive the intellectual soul to be united
through the sentient faculty with the body,
which it quickeneth. If a man's intellectual
soul should stay from quickening the body
without being separated from the body, that
man would be dead, because life would cease:
and yet his body would not be separated from

life since the intellect is his life. 'Tis as when
a man, who had attentively sought by means
of his sight to discern someone approaching,
becometh rapt in other thoughts and so withdraweth his attention from that pursuit, though
his eyes are none the less directed toward it—
that man's eye is not then separated from his
mind, although it existeth in separation from
the mind's discerning attention. But if that
state of being rapt should not only cease
quickening his discernment but should also
cease quickening his senses, his eye would be
dead because it would not be quickened. Howbeit, for all that, it would not be separated
from the intellectual form, which is the form
that giveth being, just as a withered hand
remaineth united unto the form which maketh
the whole body one.

There are men, so Saint Austin saith, who
have skill to withdraw the lifegiving spirit
from their body, and appear dead and
without feeling. In such a case, the intellectual
nature would remain united unto the body,
because that body would not exist under another form than afore: nay more, it would
not only have the same form and remain the
same body, while the quickening power would
not cease to exist, but it would remain in

union with the intellectual nature, albeit that
did not actually extend itself unto the body.
I perceive a man in such a case as one truly
dead because he lacketh the quickening life
(death being the lack of that which quickeneth), and yet he would not be a dead body
separated from its life, which is its soul.

'Tis thus, Jesu most merciful, that I look
upon the absolute life, which is God, in-
separably united unto Thy human intellect
and thereby unto Thy body. For that union
is such that none can be closer. Every union
that can be disparted is far inferior to that
than which none can be closer. Wherefore it
never was true nor can it ever be that Thy
divine nature was separated from Thy human
nature, nor yet from Thy mind nor Thy body,
the parts without which human nature cannot exist. Although it be most true that Thy
soul did cease from quickening Thy body and
that Thou didst truly undergo death, yet wast
Thou never separated from true life. If that
priest of whom Austin telleth had some kind
of power of withdrawing from the body that
which quickeneth, and attracting it into the
soul—as if a candle illumining a room were
a living thing, and should attract to the centre
of its light the beams whereby it illumined the

room, without being separated from the room,
and this attraction were naught else than
ceasing to shed forth those beams—what marvel,
then, if Thou, Jesu, hadst the power (since
Thou art the most free of living Lights), of
assuming and of laying down Thy quickening
soul? When Thou willedst to lay it down Thou
didst suffer death, and when Thou willedst to
resume it Thou didst rise again in Thine own
might.

Now the intellectual nature, when it quickeneth or animateth the body, is called the human
soul. And the soul is said to be removed when
the human intellect ceaseth to quicken it. For
when the intellect ceaseth from its function of
quickening, and, with regard to that, separateth
itself from the body, it is not therefore separated
purely and simply.

These thoughts Thou inspirest, Jesu, that Thou
mayest show Thyself unto me, most unworthy,
in so far as I can receive it, and that I may
contemplate how in Thee mortal human nature
put on immortality, so that all men sharing
that same human nature may in Thee attain
to resurrection and divine life. What can be
sweeter, what more delightsome, than to know
that in Thee, Jesu, we find all things that be
in our nature—in Thee, who alone canst do

all things, and givest most liberally and up-braidest not? O ineffable lovingkindness and mercy! Thou, God, who art goodness' self, couldest not satisfy Thine infinite clemency and bounty unless Thou gavest us Thyself! Nor could this be done more beseemingly, more possibly, for us recipients than in Thy taking on Thee our nature, because we could not approach unto Thine. Thus Thou camest unto us, and art called Jesus, our Saviour ever blessed.

CHAPTER XXIV

How Jesus is the Word of Life

Of Thine own best and greatest gift, my Jesus, I contemplate Thee preaching words of life, and plentifully sowing the seed divine in the hearts of them that hear Thee. I see those depart from Thee who have not perceived the things that are of the Spirit. But I see the disciples remaining, who have already begun to taste the sweetness of the doctrine that quickeneth the soul. On behalf of all these, that prince and leader of all the Apostles, Peter, confessed how Thou, Jesu, haddest the words of life, and marvelled that seekers after life should depart from Thee. Paul in ecstasy heard from Thee, Jesu, the words of life, and thereafter neither persecution, nor sword, nor bodily hunger could separate him from Thee. None could depart from Thee who had tasted the words of life. Who can separate a bear from honey after he hath once tasted the sweetness thereof? How great is the sweetness of truth which maketh life delightsome to the full! It surpasseth all bodily sweetness, for 'tis abso-lute sweetness, whence floweth all that is

desired by every taste! What is stronger than
love, whence all that is loveable hath that for
which it is loved? If the bond of love in limitation be sometimes so strong that the fear of
death cannot sever it, how strong is the bond
when that love is tasted whence all love
springeth? I wonder not that their cruel tor-
ments were accounted as naught by other of
Thy soldiers, Jesu, to whom Thou hadst
afforded a foretaste of Thyself, the Life. O
Jesu my Love, Thou hast sowed the seed of
life in the field of the faithful, and hast watered
it by the witness of Thy blood, and hast shown
by bodily death that truth is the life of the
rational spirit; the seed grew in good soil and
bore fruit.

Thou showest me, Lord, how my soul is the
breath of life in regard to my body, where-
into it breatheth and infuseth life, but 'tis not
life in regard to Thee, O God, but as it were a
potentiality of life. Now, Thou canst not but
grant our petitions if they be made in most
expectant faith. And so Thou dost inspire me
with the thought that there is a soul in the
child which hath vegetative power in actual
exercise, since the child groweth; he hath also
a percipient power in actual exercise, since the
child feeleth; he hath moreover an imaginative

power, but not as yet in actual exercise; and a reasoning power, the exercise whereof is as yet still more remote; he hath, too, an intellectual power, but that is even more delayed in developing. Thus we find that one and the same soul hath the lower powers in actual exercise first, and afterward the higher, as if man were animal before he is spiritual.

In the same way, we find that a certain mineral power, which can also be called spirit, existeth in the bowels of the earth, and hath the power to become a mineral of stone, or hath the power to become salt, or, again, the power to become a metal, and that there are divers such spirits in that stones, salts and metals are diverse. Howbeit, there is but one spirit of the mineral of gold, which, being ever more and more refined through the influence of the sun or sky, is at last fashioned into gold of such a nature that it may not be corrupted by any element. And 'tis in it most chiefly that the heavenly incorruptible light shineth forth, for it much resembleth the sun's corporeal light. We find the same of the vegetative spirit and of the percipient spirit. The percipient spirit, in man, conformeth itself closely unto the motive and influential power of the heavens, under which influence it

receiveth one increase after another, until it is
set in perfect act. But as 'tis drawn out from
the power of the body, its perfection ceaseth
with the failing of the bodily perfection whereon
it dependeth.

There is, finally, an intellectual spirit which,
in the act of its perfection, is independent of
the body, but is united thereunto by means of
the percipient power; this spirit, being independent of the body, is not subject unto the
influence of the heavenly bodies; 'tis independent of the percipient spirit, and thus of the
motive power of the heavens. But, just as the
motive forces of the heavenly bodies are subject unto the First Mover, so too is this moving
force, which is the intellect. Howbeit, since
'tis united unto the body by means of the
percipient power, it cometh not to perfection
without the senses, since all that reacheth it
from the world of sense doth so by the medium
of the senses. Whence naught of this kind can
exist in the intellect that hath not first existed
in the senses, but the more the senses are pure
and perfect, the imagination clear, and the
discursive reason [1] in good state, the more
the intellect in its intellectual operations is
unhampered, and clear-sighted.

[1] *discursus.*

But the intellect feedeth on the Word of life, under whose influence it is stablished, like the motive forces of the orbs; howbeit in other fashion, as even the spirits which are subject unto the influences of the heavens come to perfection in divers ways. And the intellect is not perfected, save incidentally, by the percipient spirit, just as an image maketh not perfect, albeit it stirreth up an inquiry after the truth of the exemplar. The image of the Crucified, for example, doth not inspire devotion, but kindleth the memory that devotion may be inspired. Since the intellectual spirit is not constrained by the influence of the heavens, but is absolutely free, it cometh not to perfection unless it submit itself through faith unto the Word of God, like a free disciple, under no control, who is not perfected unless by faith he submit himself unto the word of a master: he needs must have confidence in the master and listen unto him. The intellect is perfected by the Word of God, and groweth, and becometh continually more receptive and apt, and liker unto the Word.

This perfection, which thus cometh from the Word whence it had being, is not a corruptible perfection, but Godlike. Like the perfection of gold, 'tis not corruptible, but of heavenly form.

But it behoveth every intellect to submit itself by faith unto the Word of God, and to hear with closest attention that inward teaching of the supreme Master, and by hearing what the Lord saith in it it shall be made perfect. 'Twas for this that Thou, Jesu, one and only Master, didst preach the necessity of faith for all approaching the fount of life, and didst show that the inflowing of divine power was according unto the measure of faith.

Two things only hast Thou taught, O Saviour Christ—faith and love. By faith, the intellect hath access unto the Word; by love, 'tis united thereunto; the nearer it approacheth, the more it waxeth in power; the more it loveth, the more it stablisheth itself in its light. And the Word of God is within it, it needeth not to seek outside itself, since it will find Him within, and shall have access unto Him by faith. And by prayer it shall obtain a nearer approach unto Him, for the Word will increase faith by communication of His light.

I render Thee thanks, Jesu, that by Thy light I have come thus far. In Thy light I see the light of my life. I see how Thou, the Word, infusest life into all believers, and makest perfect all that love Thee. What teaching, good Jesu, was ever briefer and more effectual than

Thine? Thou persuadest us but to believe, Thou biddest us but to love. What is easier than to believe in God? What is sweeter than to love Him? How pleasant is Thy yoke, how light is Thy burden, Thou one and only Teacher! To them that obey this teaching Thou dost promise all their desires, for Thou requirest naught difficult to a believer, and naught that a lover can refuse. Such are the promises that Thou makest unto Thy disciples, and they are entirely true, for Thou art the truth, who canst promise naught but truth. Nay more, 'tis naught other than Thyself that Thou dost promise, who art the perfection of all that may be made perfect. To Thee be praise, to Thee be glory, to Thee the rendering of thanks through endless ages! Amen.

CHAPTER XXV

How Jesus is the Consummation

WHAT is it, Lord, that Thou conveyest to the spirit of the man whom Thou makest perfect? Is it not Thy good Spirit, who in His Being is consummately the power of all powers and the perfection of the perfect, since it is He that worketh all things? 'Tis as when the sun's strength, descending on the spirit of growing things, moveth it toward perfection, so that by the right pleasant and natural mellowing of the heavenly heat it may become good fruit on a good tree: even so Thy Spirit, O God, cometh upon the intellectual spirit of a good man, and, by the heat of divine love, melloweth its latent power toward perfection, that it may become fruit most acceptable unto Him.

Lord, we find that Thy One Spirit, infinite in power, is received in manifold ways, for It is received in one way by one, in whom It produceth the spirit of prophecy, and in another way by another, in whom It produceth skill in interpretation, and by yet another, to whom It teacheth knowledge, and so in divers ways in others. For His gifts are diverse, and they are perfections of the intellectual spirit, even as that same heat of the sun bringeth to perfection divers fruits on divers trees.

I perceive, Lord, that Thy Spirit cannot be lacking unto any spirit, because It is the Spirit of spirits, and motion of motions, and It filleth the whole world: but It directeth all such things as have not an intellectual spirit by means of intellectual nature which moveth the heavens and, by their motion, all things that exist thereunder. But the disposition and distribution of intellectual nature He reserved for Himself alone. For He hath espoused unto Himself this nature, wherein He chose to rest as in an house of abiding and in the heaven of truth: since 'tis intellectual nature alone that can grasp truth of itself.

Thou, Lord, who makest all things for Thine own sake, hast created this whole world for the sake of intellectual nature. Even so a painter mixeth divers colours that at length he may be able to paint himself, so that he may possess his own likeness, wherein his art may rest and take pleasure, and so that, his single self being not to be multiplied, he may at least be multiplied in the one way possible, to wit, in a

likeness most resembling himself. But the Spirit
maketh many figures, because the likeness of
His infinite power can only be perfectly set
forth in many, and they are all intellectual
spirits, serviceable to every spirit. For, were
they not innumerable, Thou, infinite God,
couldst not be known in the best fashion. For
every intellectual spirit perceiveth in Thee,
my God, somewhat which must be revealed
unto others in order that they may attain unto
Thee, their God, in the best possible fashion.
Wherefore these spirits, full of love, reveal
one unto another their secrets, and thereby
the knowledge of the Beloved is increased,
and yearning toward Him is aflame, and
sweetness of joy.

Yet, O Lord God, Thou couldst not have
brought Thy work to perfect consummation
without Thy Son, Jesus, whom Thou hast
anointed above His fellows, who is the Christ.
In His intellect the perfection of creatable
nature is at rest, for He is the final and entirely
perfect Image of God who cannot be multiplied, and there can be but one such supreme
Image. Howbeit, all other intellectual spirits
are, through the medium of that Spirit, likenesses, and the more perfect the more they
resemble It. And all rest in that Spirit as in

the final perfection of the Image of God, of whose Image they have attained the likeness, and some degree of perfection.

Wherefore of Thy giving, O my God, I possess this whole visible world and all the Scripture, and all ministering spirits to aid me to advance in knowledge of Thee. Yea, all things stir me up to turn unto Thee: all Scriptures strive only to set Thee forth, and all intellectual spirits exercise themselves only in seeking Thee and in revealing as much of Thee as they have found. Thou hast above all given me Jesus as Master, as the Way, the Truth, and the Life, so that absolutely nothing may be lacking unto me. Thou dost strengthen me by Thy Holy Spirit, through Him Thou dost inspire the choice of life, holy yearnings. Thou dost draw me, by a foretaste of the sweetness of the life in glory, to love Thee, O infinite Good! Thou dost ravish me above myself that I may foresee the glorious place whereunto Thou callest me. For Thou showest me many dainties most delectable, that allure me by their excellent savour: Thou grantest me to behold the treasury of riches, of life, of joy, of beauty. Thou uncoverest the fountain whence floweth all that is desirable alike in nature and in art. Thou keepest naught secret. Thou hidest not the channel of love, of peace, and of rest. All things dost Thou set before me, a miserable creature whom Thou didst create from nothing.

Why then do I delay, why do I not run, in the sweet smell of the unguents of my Christ? Why do I not enter into the joy of my Lord? What restraineth me? If ignorance of Thee, Lord, hath held me back, and the empty delight of the world of sense, they shall restrain me no longer. For I desire, Lord (since Thou grantest me so to desire) to leave the things of this world, because the world desireth to leave me. I hasten toward the goal, I have all but finished my course, I will be beforehand with it in taking farewell, I who pant for my crown. Draw me, Lord, for none can come unto Thee save he be drawn by Thee; grant that, thus drawn, I may be set free from this world and may be united unto Thee, the absolute God, in an eternity of glorious life.

AMEN.

THE END OF THE BOOK OF THE VISION OF GOD

COSIMO is a specialty publisher of books and publications that inspire, inform and engage readers. Our mission is to offer unique books to niche audiences around the world.

COSIMO CLASSICS offers a collection of distinctive titles by the great authors and thinkers throughout the ages. At COSIMO CLASSICS timeless classics find a new life as affordable books, covering a variety of subjects including: *Biographies, Business, History, Mythology, Personal Development, Philosophy, Religion and Spirituality,* and much more!

COSIMO-on-DEMAND publishes books and publications for innovative authors, non-profit organizations and businesses. COSIMO-on-DEMAND specializes in bringing books back into print, publishing new books quickly and effectively, and making these publications available to readers around the world.

COSIMO REPORTS publishes public reports that affect your world: from global trends to the economy, and from health to geo-politics.

FOR MORE INFORMATION CONTACT US AT
INFO@COSIMOBOOKS.COM

✻ If you are a book-lover interested in our current catalog of books.

✻ If you are an author who wants to get published

✻ If you represent an organization or business seeking to reach your members, donors or customers with your own books and publications

**COSIMO BOOKS ARE ALWAYS
AVAILABLE AT ONLINE BOOKSTORES**

VISIT COSIMOBOOKS.COM
BE INSPIRED, BE INFORMED

Made in the USA
Monee, IL
17 December 2023

49625273R00100